Time is Running Out

By
Shaykh Mufti Saiful Islām

JKN Publications

© Copyright by JKN Publications

First Published in May 2020

ISBN 978-1-909114-60-9

British Library Cataloguing in Publication Data
A catalogue record for this book is available from the British Library.

Publisher's Note:

Every care and attention has been put into the production of this book. If however, you find any errors they are our own, for which we seek Allāh's ﷻ forgiveness and the reader's pardon.

Published by:

JKN Publications
118 Manningham Lane
Bradford
West Yorkshire
BD8 7JF
United Kingdom

t: +44 (0) 1274 308 456 | w: www.jkn.org.uk | e: info@jkn.org.uk

Book Title: Time is Running Out

Author: Shaykh Mufti Saiful Islām

Printed by Mega Printing in Turkey

"In the Name of Allāh, the Most Beneficent,
the Most Merciful"

Contents

Contents

Sūrah Zilzāl (99)
In the name of Allāh ﷻ, the Beneficent, the Merciful.

إِذَا زُلْزِلَتِ الْأَرْضُ زِلْزَالَهَا ٥

(1) When the earth shall quake most violently.

وَأَخْرَجَتِ الْأَرْضُ أَثْقَالَهَا ٥

(2) When the earth will throw up loads of (dead bodies and treasures).

وَقَالَ الْإِنْسَانُ مَا لَهَا ٥

(3) And men will ask, "What is the matter with her?

يَوْمَئِذٍ تُحَدِّثُ أَخْبَارَهَا ٥

(4) On that day she will narrate her stories.

بِأَنَّ رَبَّكَ أَوْحَىٰ لَهَا ٥

(5) Because your Lord will command her to do so.

يَوْمَئِذٍ يَصْدُرُ النَّاسُ أَشْتَاتًا لِيُرَوْا أَعْمَالَهُمْ ٥

(6) On that day people will return in different groups to witness their actions.

فَمَنْ يَعْمَلْ مِثْقَالَ ذَرَّةٍ خَيْرًا يَرَهُ ٥

(7) Whoever has done an atom's weight of good will see it.

وَمَنْ يَعْمَلْ مِثْقَالَ ذَرَّةٍ شَرًّا يَرَهُ ٥

(8) And whoever has done an atom's weight of evil will see it.

Connection Between the Previous Sūrah and the Present Sūrah

In the previous Sūrah (Sūrah Bayyinah), Allāh ﷻ mentioned,

جَزَاؤُهُمْ عِنْدَ رَبِّهِمْ جَنَّاتُ عَدْنٍ تَجْرِي مِنْ تَحْتِهَا الْأَنْهَارُ خَالِدِينَ فِيهَا أَبَدًا

**"Their reward with their Lord is eternal Paradise where they
shall live forever and ever..."(98:8)**

Hence, the Believers after hearing the glad-tidings will have the zeal
and enthusiasm and will anticipate to receive these great blessings.
Allāh ﷻ informs us in the present Sūrah that His glad-tidings and
presentation will be on the Day of Judgement. Furthermore, Allāh
ﷻ explains the horrors of Judgement Day and it's catastrophic
scenes.

Also in the previous Sūrah, Allāh ﷻ illustrated the guideline for the
fortunate individuals and that is the fear of Allāh ﷻ:

ذٰلِكَ لِمَنْ خَشِيَ رَبَّهُ ۚ ٨

(8)"...This (reward) is for him who fears his Lord."

Now in this present Sūrah, Allāh ﷻ informs mankind the time for
the result of a fortunate individual and a wicked individual which
will become manifest on the Day of Reckoning. On that Day, everyone will see the outcome and effect of their deeds.

Shān-e-Nuzūl: Cause of Revelation

Some commentators have stated that a very eloquent and articulate poet of Arabic composed this sentence:

إِذَا زُلْزِلَتِ الْأَرْضُ زِلْزَالًا

The Qur'anic verse was revealed:

إِذَا زُلْزِلَتِ الْأَرْضُ زِلْزَالَهَاۙ
(1) When the earth shall quake most violently.

After hearing the Qur'anic verse, he became ecstatic that the word زِلْزَالًا (which he used) is only a Masdar (root word) which is insufficient in describing the magnanimity of the quake. When the Qur'ān explained it with إِضَافَت (joining the word زِلْزَال - quake) with the earth, then it created that tremendous eloquence and grammatical emphasis of greatness that cannot be explained in words. The poet spontaneously exclaimed, "I bring faith on the Holy Qur'ān.

Virtues of Sūrah Zilzāl

Sayyidunā Abdullāh Ibn Abbās ؓ narrates from the Holy Prophet ﷺ that Sūrah Zilzāl equals half of the Holy Qur'ān, Sūrah Ikhlās equals a third of the Holy Qur'ān and Sūrah Kāfirūn equals a quarter of the Holy Qur'ān. (Tirmizī)

Sayyidunā Anas ﷺ narrates that the Messenger of Allāh ﷺ once asked someone whether he was married. When the person replied that he was unable to marry because he did not have the means, Rasūlullāh ﷺ asked him whether he knew Sūrah Ikhlās. When he replied in the affirmative, Rasūlullāh ﷺ told him that Sūrah Ikhlās equalled a quarter of the Holy Qur'ān. Thereafter, Rasūlullāh ﷺ asked him whether he knew Sūrah Zilzāl. When he replied in the affirmative, Rasūlullāh ﷺ told him that Sūrah Zilzāl equalled a quarter of the Holy Qur'ān. He then instructed him to marry, telling him that Allāh ﷺ would get him married by the blessings of the Sūrahs. (Ibn Kathīr)

There is no contradiction between the narrations that place the reward of Sūrah Zilzāl as a quarter of the Holy Qur'ān and those that place the reward as half of the Holy Qur'ān because it is possible that Allāh ﷺ increased the reward from a quarter to a half. The same applies to the reward of Sūrah Ikhlās which is placed at a quarter as well as a third of the Holy Qur'ān.

Hence in the narration of Sayyidunā Anas Ibn Mālik ﷺ it states that the Holy Prophet ﷺ said, "Whoever recites Sūrah Zilzāl, it would be equal for him (in reward) of one half of the Holy Qur'ān and whoever recites Sūrah Ikhlās, it would be equal for him (in reward) of one third of the Holy Qur'ān." (Tirmizī)

Sayyidunā Abdullāh Ibn Amr ﷺ said, "A man came to the Holy Prophet ﷺ and said, 'Direct me to recite O Rasūlullāh ﷺ!' The Holy

Prophet ﷺ said to the man,

اِقْرَأْ ثَلَاثًا مِنْ ذَوَاتِ الٓرٰ

'Recite three Sūrahs from those (which begin) with the letter Alif, Lām, Rā.' The man said, 'I have become old and my tongue has become heavy.' The Holy Prophet ﷺ said,

فَاقْرَأْ مِنْ ذَوَاتِ حٰمٓ

'Then recite three Sūrahs with the letters Hā-Mīm.'

The man said something similar to his previous statement. Then the Holy Prophet ﷺ said,

اِقْرَأْ ثَلَاثًا مِنَ الْمُسَبِّحَاتِ

'Recite three from the Musabbihāt (glorification Sūrahs).'

The man repeated his previous statement and said, 'Show me how to recite a comprehensive Sūrah.' The Holy Prophet ﷺ showed him how to recite Sūrah Zilzāl and when he reached the end of the Sūrah the man said, 'By He Who has sent you with the truth as a Prophet, I will never add anything else to it.' Then the man turned away and left, and the Holy Prophet ﷺ said,

اَفْلَحَ الرُّجَيْلُ اَفْلَحَ الرُّجَيْلُ

The little man has become successful, the little man has become successful.'" (Ibn Mājah)

Commentary: Earthquake

It is not clear whether the convulsion in the world will take place before the first blowing of the trumpet as is mentioned in connection with the portents of the Doomsday, or it may be referring to the quake that will occur after the second blowing, when the dead bodies will be resurrected and thrown out of their graves. Narratives and views of the commentators differ on this issue.

According to different traditions, many quakes and convulsions would occur: first, before the first blowing; and second, after the second blowing, at the time of raising the dead. Here it most likely refers to the second quake, and context supports it, because the Sūrah later on describes the scenes of the Day of Resurrection, such as reckoning, weighing and evaluating of deeds and recompense.

Nevertheless, this earthquake shall be extremely severe, as Allāh ﷻ mentions in the first two verses of Sūrah Hajj,

يَا أَيُّهَا النَّاسُ اتَّقُوا رَبَّكُمْ إِنَّ زَلْزَلَةَ السَّاعَةِ شَيْءٌ عَظِيمٌ ۞ يَوْمَ تَرَوْنَهَا تَذْهَلُ كُلُّ مُرْضِعَةٍ عَمَّا أَرْضَعَتْ وَتَضَعُ كُلُّ ذَاتِ حَمْلٍ حَمْلَهَا وَتَرَى النَّاسَ سُكَارَىٰ وَمَا هُمْ بِسُكَارَىٰ وَلَٰكِنَّ عَذَابَ اللّٰهِ شَدِيدٌ ۝

"O People! Fear your Lord. The earthquake of Qiyāmah is a tremendous thing indeed. The day when you will witness it, every nursing mother will forget her suckling infant and every pregnant woman will abort her pregnancy. And you will see people

in a drunken state although they will not be drunk, but Allāh's punishment is severe." (22:1-2)

This earthquake will affect not only a few towns or a country, but the entire earth.

After the convulsion of the earth, corpses will be raised from their graves and ushered to the plain of resurrection. Allāh ﷻ says that on the Day of Judgement,

وَأَخْرَجَتِ الْأَرْضُ أَثْقَالَهَا ۞ وَقَالَ الْإِنْسَانُ مَا لَهَا

(1-2) "The earth will remove her load and man will ask, 'What is the matter with her?"

On the Day of Qiyāmah, the earth will empty her belly of all the dead and the treasures she concealed beneath her surface. However, all this wealth will not benefit anyone. The same wealth for which man killed his brothers will now lie useless.

When man will stand for reckoning before Allāh ﷻ, he will be given his record of deeds and witnesses will attest to the deeds he committed. Among those witnesses will be the earth. Referring to this, Allāh ﷻ says, **"On that day, she will narrate her stories because your Lord will command her to do so. When the earth will do this, man will be astonished and ask, 'What is the matter with her (i.e. we thought she was lifeless, how is it that she now talks)?' The earth will talk on the Day of Judgement 'Because**

your Lord will command her to do so.'" (3-5)

Just as Allāh ﷻ gave speech to the tongue, Allāh ﷻ will give speech to man's limbs, as well as to the earth so that they may testify against people.

Sayyidunā Abū Hurairah ؓ narrates that the Holy Prophet ﷺ once recited the verse,

$$يَوْمَئِذٍ تُحَدِّثُ أَخْبَارَهَا ٥$$

(4) "On that day she will narrate her stories."

and then he asked the Sahābah ؓ,

$$أَتَدْرُونَ مَا أَخْبَارُهَا؟$$

"Do you know what her stories are?"

The Sahābah ؓ submitted, "Allāh ﷻ and His Rasūl ﷺ know best." The Prophet ﷺ then told the Sahābah ؓ,

$$فَإِنَّ أَخْبَارَهَا أَنْ تَشْهَدَ عَلَى كُلِّ عَبْدٍ وَأَمَةٍ بِمَا عَمِلَ عَلَى ظَهْرِهَا أَنْ تَقُوْلَ: عَمِلَ كَذَا وَكَذَا يَوْمَ$$
$$كَذَا وَكَذَا فَهٰذِهِ أَخْبَارُهَا$$

"Verily, it's stories are that it will testify against every male and female servant, about what they did upon it's surface. It will say that he did such and such on such and such day. So this is it's stories and information."

Four Witnesses

When a person commits a sin, immediately four witnesses stand against him:

1. Kirāman Kātibīn - the two angels on his both sides writing all of his good and bad deeds. The Holy Qur'ān says:

$$كِرَامًا كَاتِبِينَ ۞ يَعْلَمُونَ مَا تَفْعَلُونَ ۝$$

"(Angels) who are noble and are recording. They know what you do." (81: 1-2)

2. His body parts and limbs. The Holy Qur'ān says,

$$اَلْيَوْمَ نَخْتِمُ عَلَى أَفْوَاهِهِمْ وَتُكَلِّمُنَا أَيْدِيهِمْ وَتَشْهَدُ أَرْجُلُهُمْ بِمَا كَانُوا يَكْسِبُونَ ۝$$

"On this day We shall seal their mouths. Their hands will speak to Us and their legs will testify to what they earned." (36:65)

3. The Book of Records. Allāh ﷻ says,

$$وَإِذَا الصُّحُفُ نُشِرَتْ ۝$$

"When the Book of Records will be opened." (81:10)

In a verse of Sūrah Banī Isrā'īl, Allāh ﷻ says,

وَكُلَّ إِنسَانٍ أَلْزَمْنَاهُ طَائِرَهُ فِي عُنُقِهِ وَنُخْرِجُ لَهُ يَوْمَ الْقِيَامَةِ كِتَابًا يَلْقَاهُ مَنشُورًا ۞ اقْرَأْ

كِتَابَكَ كَفَى بِنَفْسِكَ الْيَوْمَ عَلَيْكَ حَسِيبًا ○

"We have bound every person's actions on his neck. On the Day of Judgement, We shall take out for him a book that he will see opened before him, (It will be said to him) 'Read your book, today you are enough to take stock of yourself."(17:13-16)

4.   And finally the earth will be a witness as mentioned earlier.

يَوْمَئِذٍ تُحَدِّثُ أَخْبَارَهَا

(4) That day it will declare it's information.

So the question is, when a person perpetrates a sin then these four strong opponents stand against him as witnesses - then how does he save himself? The Holy Prophet ﷺ has told us a prescription and that is sincere Tawbah (repentance).

Hakīmul-Ummah Shaykh Ashraf Ali Thānwi ﷫ mentions a Hadīth from Jāmi' Saghīr:

When a servant of Allāh ﷻ carries out sincere Tawbah, then Allāh ﷻ makes the angels (Kirāman Kātibīn) forget his sins. He even eradicates the signs and marks from the ground until he meets Allāh ﷻ on the Day of Judgement, in the state that he will have no witness against him.

Subhān-Allāh! May Allāh ﷻ make us from the sincere and the true repenters. Āmīn!

Two Groups

Allāh ﷻ says in verse 6:

يَوْمَئِذٍ يَّصْدُرُ النَّاسُ أَشْتَاتًا لِّيُرَوْا أَعْمَالَهُمْ ۟

(6) "On that day people will return in different groups to witness their actions."

After completing their reckoning, people will be separated into two groups. Those destined for Jannah will be led to a road on the right of the plains of resurrection, while those destined for Jahannam will be led to a road on the left.

It is with reference to this that Allāh ﷻ mentions in Sūrah Rūm,

وَيَوْمَ تَقُوْمُ السَّاعَةُ يَوْمَئِذٍ يَّتَفَرَّقُوْنَ ۞ فَأَمَّا الَّذِيْنَ آمَنُوْا وَعَمِلُوا الصَّالِحَاتِ فَهُمْ فِيْ رَوْضَةٍ يُّحْبَرُوْنَ ۞ وَأَمَّا الَّذِيْنَ كَفَرُوْا وَكَذَّبُوْا بِآيَاتِنَا وَلِقَاءِ الْآخِرَةِ فَأُوْلٰئِكَ فِي الْعَذَابِ مُحْضَرُوْنَ ۟

"That day when Qiyāmah will dawn, that day they will be in different conditions. As for those who believe and do good deeds, they will be rejoicing in a garden. As for those who disbelieve and falsify Our signs and the meeting of the Hereafter, these people will be exposed to punishment." (30:14-16)

Concerning the same two groups of people on the Day of Judgement, Allāh ﷻ says in Sūrah Zumar,

وَسِيْقَ الَّذِيْنَ كَفَرُوْا إِلَى جَهَنَّمَ زُمَرًا

"The disbelievers will be dragged into Jahannam in groups..."(39:71)

and

وَسِيْقَ الَّذِيْنَ كَفَرُوْا إِلَى الْجَنَّةِ زُمَرًا

"Those who feared their Lord will be lead to Jannah in groups." (39:73)

The Day of Judgement will be frightful when people will be separated into these two groups and the sinners will be told,

وَامْتَازُوا الْيَوْمَ أَيُّهَا الْمُجْرِمُوْنَ

(59) "Separate yourselves today, O you criminals."

The pious will then be left on their own to enter happily into Jannah. Allāh ﷻ says that the two groups will proceed to "witness their deeds (لِّيَرَوْا أَعْمَالَهُمْ)." That is, to witness the consequences of their deeds; either Jannah or Jahannam.

Most Comprehensive Verse

The concluding two verses of the Sūrah though brief are extremely comprehensive. Allāh ﷻ declares,

فَمَنْ يَّعْمَلْ مِثْقَالَ ذَرَّةٍ خَيْرًا يَّرَهٗ ۝

(7) "Whoever has done an iota weight of good will see it (i.e. it's reward)."

and

وَمَنْ يَّعْمَلْ مِثْقَالَ ذَرَّةٍ شَرًّا يَّرَهٗ ۝

(8) "And whoever has done an iota weight of evil will see it (i.e. will see it's punishment)"

These verses make it clear that no good deed should be overlooked and no sin should be committed thinking it to be insignificant, because one will eventually see the consequences of every deed.

The Prophet ﷺ was once explaining the details of Zakāt to the Saḥābah ﷺ when someone asked about the Zakāt due from a person who owns donkeys. He replied,

لَمْ يُنْزَلْ عَلَيَّ فِيهَا شَيْءٌ إِلَّا هٰذِهِ الْآيَةُ الْجَامِعَةُ الْفَاذَّةُ فَمَنْ يَّعْمَلْ مِثْقَالَ ذَرَّةٍ خَيْرًا يَّرَهٗ وَمَنْ يَّعْمَلْ مِثْقَالَ ذَرَّةٍ شَرًّا يَّرَهٗ

"Although no specific law has been revealed to me concerning the Zakāt of donkeys, a most comprehensive verse has been revealed to me, "Whoever does an atoms weight of good will see it and whoever does an atoms weight of evil will see it." (Bukhāri)

A person who is concerned about his life in the Hereafter should never allow an opportunity to do a good deed pass by him. He seizes every such opportunity and even the moment in which he can recite Subhān-Allāh once is not forfeited.

Sayyidunā Adi Ibn Hātim ﷺ narrates that the Holy Prophet ﷺ said,

إِتَّقُوا النَّارَ وَلَوْ بِشِقِّ تَمْرَةٍ فَمَنْ لَّمْ يَجِدْ فَبِكَلِمَةٍ طَيِّبَةٍ

Fear (ward off) the fire, even by giving half a date in charity, and even by saying a single word of good. (Bukhāri)

Sayyidunā Umar ﷺ narrates that the Holy Prophet ﷺ was once delivering a sermon when he said, "Behold! This world is a cash commodity from which good and evil eat. Behold! The promise of the Hereafter (although not cash) is absolutely true. The All Powerful Sovereign shall pass judgement there. Behold! All good shall be in Jannah and all evil shall be in Jahannam. Behold! Continue carrying out deeds, continue fearing Allāh ﷻ and remember that your deeds will be presented before you because, "Whoever does an iota weight of good will see it and whoever does an iota weight of evil will see it.

(Miskhāt)

Value Your Good Deeds

Sayyidah Āisha ‎ narrates that the Holy Prophet ‎ said to her, "Avoid even the smallest sins because Allāh ‎ has appointed those who seek them (i.e. the recording angels who record them).

(Mishkāt)

Sayyidunā Anas ‎ once told the people with him, "You people carry out deeds that you regard to be finer than a strand of hair (i.e. you regard them to be insignificant), but during the time of the Holy Prophet ‎ we would regard them to be devastating." (Bukhāri)

Hence, we should carry out every small good deed possible and never under estimate them.

لَا تَحْقِرَنَّ مِنَ الْمَعْرُوْفِ شَيْئًا وَلَوْ أَنْ تُفْرِغَ مِنْ دَلْوِكَ فِي اِنَاءِ الْمُسْتَقِي وَلَوْ أَنْ تَلْقٰى أَخَاكَ وَ وَجْهُكَ إِلَيْهِ مُنْبَسِطٌ

"Do not under estimate any good deed, even if it is offering drinking water from your bucket to one who is seeking a drink, or meeting your brother with a cheerful face." (Muslim)

In a Hadīth of Bukhāri it states,

يَا مَعْشَرَ النِّسَاءِ الْمُؤْمِنَاتِ لَا تَحْقِرَنَّ جَارَةٌ لِجَارَتِهَا وَلَوْ فِرْسَنَ شَاةٍ

"O party of believing women! None of you should belittle a gift sent from your neighbour, even if it is a hoof of a sheep." (Bukhāri)

In another Hadīth it says,

رُدُّوا السَّائِلَ وَلَوْ بِظُلْفٍ مُحَرَّقٍ

"Give something to the beggar, even if it is a burnt hoof."

The Holy Prophet ﷺ made a parable of them (sins that are taken lightly) by saying that they are like a group of people who settle in barren land. Then their leader comes and orders the men to go out one at a time and each bring back a stick until they have gathered a large number of sticks. Then they kindle a fire and burn everything that they threw in it." (Ahmad)

The concluding two verses according to Sayyidunā Abdullāh Ibn Mas'ūd ﷺ are the most robust and comprehensive verses of the Holy Qur'ān. Sayyidunā Anas ﷺ as mentioned earlier reported from the Holy Prophet ﷺ that these verses are the most unique and comprehensive verses of the Holy Qur'ān.

Sūrah Ādiyāt (100)

In the name of Allāh, the Beneficent, the Merciful.

وَالْعَادِيَاتِ ضَبْحًا ٥

(1)   By (the oath of) the horses that pant as they gallop!

فَالْمُورِيَاتِ قَدْحًا ٥

(2)   By the sparks that fly from the striking of their hooves.

فَالْمُغِيرَاتِ صُبْحًا ٥

(3)   By their attack of dawn.

فَأَثَرْنَ بِهِ نَقْعًا ٥

(4)   Causing the dust to fly.

فَوَسَطْنَ بِهِ جَمْعًا ٥

(5)   And penetrating the midst of the enemy's rank.

إِنَّ الْإِنْسَانَ لِرَبِّهِ لَكَنُودٌ ٥

(6)   Indeed man is extremely ungrateful to his Lord.

وَإِنَّهُ عَلَى ذٰلِكَ لَشَهِيدٌ ٥

(7)   Indeed, he (man) is also a witness to this fact.

وَإِنَّهُ لِحُبِّ الْخَيْرِ لَشَدِيدٌ ٥

(8)   Verily he has a profound love for wealth.

أَفَلَا يَعْلَمُ إِذَا بُعْثِرَ مَا فِي الْقُبُورِ ٥

(9)   Is he not aware of the time when whatever lies within the graves shall be raised.

وَحُصِّلَ مَا فِي الصُّدُورِ ٥

(10) And whatever lies within the chests will be exposed.

إِنَّ رَبَّهُم بِهِمْ يَوْمَئِذٍ لَّخَبِيرٌ ٥

(11) On that day, their Lord will be fully aware of them.

Place of Revelation

There is a difference of opinion regarding the place of revelation.

According to Sayyidunā Abdullāh Ibn Mas'ūd ؓ, Sayyidunā Jābir ؓ, Hasan Basri ؒ, Ikrimah ؒ and Atā ؓ, Sūrah Ādiyāt was revealed in Makkah.

On the other hand, Sayyidunā Abdullāh Ibn Abbās ؓ, Sayyidunā Anas ؓ, Imām Mālik ؒ and Qatādah ؒ say that the Sūrah was revealed in Madīnah. (Qurtubi)

Allāh ﷻ takes oath by five attributes of horses to emphasise the subject matter - the fact that man is extremely ungrateful to Allāh ﷻ.

Connection between the previous Sūrah and the present Sūrah

In Sūrah Zilzāl, Allāh ﷻ mentions the general principal of compensation - whatever he commits in this world, he will need to give an account of on the Day of Judgement, whether it is an atom of good deed or bad deed.

ιe present Sūrah, Sūrah Ādiyāt, Allāh ﷻ mentions the evil traits
man for which he is despised by all and for which he ultimately
ɔrgets his Lord. He is reminded that a day will eventually come in
which he will be resurrected and he will be called for his accounts.

Subject Matter

In this Sūrah, Allāh ﷻ describes the special features of war-horses
and takes an oath by five attributes of these horses. The subject of
the oath states that man is very ungrateful to his Lord.

In this Sūrah, Allāh ﷻ describes the war-horses and their hard tasks
and efforts. By mentioning their extraordinary feats, it is bearing tes-
timony to the fact that man is very ungrateful for Allāh's ﷻ favours.
In other words, man needs to look at the horses, especially the war-
horses who risk their lives to travel under dangerous and difficult
conditions, especially in the battlefield where they follow the commands and instructions of their masters, whereas man has not created them, he has not even created the fodder he gives to them. His
duty is merely to give them the fodder that Allāh ﷻ has created. The
horses recognise and acknowledge this little favour man does to
them, and are prepared to risk their lives and bear the greatest of
hardships.

Allāh ﷻ has created man with an insignificant drop of sperm and en-
dowed him with high faculties, abilities, intellect and senses to perform various types of talks, thus making him the crown of His crea-

tion. He provides him with all types of food. Facilities are created for all his needs and necessities in an amazing manner. But man does not recognize and acknowledge any of these sublime favours, nor does he express his gratitude to his Creator.

Virtues of Sūrah Ādiyāt

Sayyidunā Hasan ؓ narrates that the Holy Prophet ﷺ said,

"Sūrah Zilzāl equals to one half of the Holy Qur'ān and Sūrah Ādiyāt is equal to one half of the Holy Qur'ān." (Tirmizī)

Grammatical Analysis

The word عَادِيَات (Ādiyāt) is derived from the root عَدْوٌ (Adw) which means to run. The word ضَبْحٌ (Dabh) means the sound coming out of the chest of a horse when it runs fast and breathes, laboriously panting. The word مُوْرِيَات (Mūriyāt) is the active participle of the infinitive إِيْرَاءٌ (Īrā). The infinitive means to strike or produce fire with a particular piece of wood. The word قَدْحٌ (Qadh) means 'to strike or produce fire with a flint; striking sparks of fire when the horse runs fast on a rocking ground with horse-shoes on. The word مُغِيْرَات (Mughīrāt) is the active participle of the infinitive إِغَارَة (Ighārah). The infinitive means to attack or make a sudden hostile excursion upon an enemy. The word صُبْحًا (Subh) means morning or dawn.

This time has been specifically mentioned because it was the practise of the Arabs to attack their enemy at dawn, and not at night in order to show off their bravery. They thought making a hostile excursion on the enemy in the darkness of night was an act of cowardice.

The word أَثَرْنَ (Atharna) is derived from إِثَارَة (Ithārah) which means to raise dust. The word نَقْعُ (Naq) means dust. This implies that the dust became stirred up and spread upon the horizon especially in the morning when the horses run fast. Normally, this is not the time for clouds of dust to fly in this way, unless it was caused by very fast running.

Verse No. 5:

فَوَسَطْنَ بِهِ جَمْعًا ⃝

'Then enter, at the same time into the centre of the enemies rank.'

In other words, they penetrate into the centre of the enemy forces without the least degree of fear.

The meaning of Kanūd

The word كَنُوْدٌ (Kanūd) according to Imām Mujāhid is اَلْكَفُوْرُ (ungrateful).

Hasan Basri ؓ says كَنُوْدٌ (Kanūd) refers to the one who counts the calamities that befall him and forgets Allāh's ﷻ favours.

Abū Bakr Wāsili ؒ said that Kanūd is the one who spends the bounties of Allāh ﷻ for sinful purposes.

Imām Tirmizī ؒ said that Kanūd is the one who looks at the bounty, and not the Bounteous Lord. In short, all these interpretations lead to the sense of ungratefulness to favours and bounties, hence the expression Kanūd means ungrateful.

Love of Wealth

Allāh ﷻ continues, **"Indeed, he (man) is also a witness to this fact."** i.e. to the fact that he is extremely ungrateful. In addition to this, **"Verily he has a profound love for wealth."**

Literally, the word خَيْر (Khair) means every good thing. In the verse it refers to wealth, implying that wealth is an embodiment of goodness and benefit. However, many a times wealth can be a disaster and calamity for mankind. This is wealth which has been acquired through unlawful means.

To recap, Allāh ﷻ takes oath by five attributes of horses to emphasise the fact firstly, man is extremely ungrateful to Allāh ﷻ and secondly, he is passionate in his love for wealth.
Both these feats and points are evil, rationally as well as from the Shar'iah point of view.
These facts warn man against these evils. The evil of ingratitude is obvious and needs no elaboration, but the evil of man's passionate love for wealth is not that obvious, and needs some elaboration.

Wealth is the axis of man's needs and necessities. Shar'iah has not only permitted its acquisition, but it has also made it's acquisition obligatory to the degree of his needs. The Holy Prophet ﷺ said,

$$ طَلَبُ كَسْبِ الْحَلَالِ فَرِيْضَةٌ بَعْدَ الْفَرِيْضَةِ $$

"Seeking a Halāl livelihood is an obligation after other obligations.
(Baihaqi)

Therefore, what is condemned in the verse is either the 'intense' or excessive love for wealth that makes one neglectful to ones obligations and oblivious of the divine injunctions, or it implies that, although earning wealth and saving it according to ones needs is permissible, having its love in the heart is bad.
Let us consider the following examples.

When man feels the need to answer the call of nature, he does it out of necessity. In fact, he makes arrangements for it, but he does not develop love or passion for it in his heart. Likewise, when he falls sick and takes medication, or even undergoes surgery, he does not develop attachment for it in his heart. He does it only out of necessity. The believer should treat the wealth in this way. A believer should acquire wealth, as Allāh ﷻ has commanded him to the extent of his need, serve it, look after it and utilize it whenever and wherever necessary, but his heart should not be attached to it. How aptly and elegantly Maulāna Rūmi ﷫ has put it in one of his couplets,

"As long as the water remains under the boat, it helps the boat (to sail); but if the water seeps into the boat, it sinks it."

Likewise, as long as the wealth floats around the boat of the heart, it would be useful; but when it seeps into the heart, it will destroy it. Allāh ﷻ concludes the Sūrah by warning mankind of the evil consequences of these two evil qualities. Everything that man conceals within his heart will be exposed on the Day of Judgement. These two evil qualities are the essential characteristics of disbelievers, and if they are found in a Muslim, he needs to reflect and be careful.

In the last verse, Allāh ﷻ reminds man that even though He is informed about the deeds and condition of his creation at all times. However, because the Day of Judgement is the day when reckoning will take place and the day when deeds will be brought to the fore,

He emphasises, **"On that day their Lord shall certainly be In-formed about them."**

Sūrah Qāri'ah
(The Knocker)
In the name of Allāh, the Most Compassionate, the Most Merciful.

اَلْقَارِعَةُ ٥

1) The knocker

مَا الْقَارِعَةُ ٥

2) What is the knocker?

وَمَا أَدْرَاكَ مَا الْقَارِعَةُ ٥

3) What shall inform you what the knocker is?

يَوْمَ يَكُوْنُ النَّاسُ كَالْفَرَاشِ الْمَبْثُوْثِ ٥

4) (It is) the day when people will become like scattered moths.

وَتَكُوْنُ الْجِبَالُ كَالْعِهْنِ الْمَنْفُوْشِ ٥

5) And the mountains will become like coloured cotton flakes of wool.

فَأَمَّا مَنْ ثَقُلَتْ مَوَازِيْنُهُ ٥

6) As for him whose scales are weighty.

فَهُوَ فِيْ عِيْشَةٍ رَّاضِيَةٍ ٥

7)   He shall be in a life of happiness.

وَأَمَّا مَنْ خَفَّتْ مَوَازِينُهُ ۟

8)   As for him whose scales are light.

فَأُمُّهُ هَاوِيَةٌ ۟

9)   His abode shall be the pit.

وَمَا أَدْرَاكَ مَا هِيَهْ ۟

10)   How will you know what this (pit) is?

نَارٌ حَامِيَةٌ ۟

11)   It is the blazing fire.

Connection Between the Previous Sūrah and the Present Sūrah

Qāri'ah is one of the names of the Day of Judgement, like Ghāshi-yah, Hāqqah, Tāmmah, Sākkhah and many other names.

This Sūrah has relevance and connection with the previous Sūrah, Sūrah Ādiyāt. Allāh ﷻ in the previous Sūrah mentions about the resurrection and concludes on the note that, on the Day of Resurrection, Allāh ﷻ our Lord shall certainly be informed of our deeds.

So it is as though the questioner is asking what is the day? Hence this Sūrah is replying to the question. The day is so intense that it will knock everyone senseless.

31

This Sūrah describes Qiyāmah as such, that it is as though someone is knocking at one's door.

Horrors of Judgement Day

When Qiyāmah comes, people will be engaged in their various activities. Some will be attending to their business and occupation, while others will be in amusement or sleeping. Qiyāmah will take place suddenly and everyone will be caught unaware, just as people are surprised by unexpected visitors at their doors.

يَسْأَلُونَكَ عَنِ السَّاعَةِ أَيَّانَ مُرْسَاهَا قُلْ إِنَّمَا عِلْمُهَا عِنْدَ رَبِّي لَا يُجَلِّيهَا لِوَقْتِهَا إِلَّا هُوَ ثَقُلَتْ فِي السَّمَاوَاتِ وَالْأَرْضِ لَا تَأْتِيكُمْ إِلَّا بَغْتَةً

Allāh says, They ask you (O Muhammad about Qiyāmah, when it will occur. Say, "The knowledge of this is only with my Lord. (only Allāh knows when it will occur). Only He will make it appear in its time. It (the occurrence of Qiyāmah) will be weighty on the heavens and the earth and will appear suddenly. (7:187)

يَسْأَلُونَكَ كَأَنَّكَ حَفِيٌّ عَنْهَا قُلْ إِنَّمَا عِلْمُهَا عِنْدَ اللهِ وَلٰكِنَّ أَكْثَرَ النَّاسِ لَا يَعْلَمُونَ

They ask you as if you have perfect knowledge of it. Say, "The knowledge of this is only with Allāh, but most people do not know. (7:187)

To emphasise the importance of the Day of Qiyāmah, it is described as the day when people will become scattered like moths. Just as moths are bewildered and dozed by a bright light and gather in confusion, people will suffer the same confusion on the Day of Qiyāmah. Allāh ﷻ uses another simile in Sūrah Qiyāmah when he says, they shall emerge from their graves as if they are scattered locust.(44:7)

Describing the condition of the mighty mountains on the Day of Qiyāmah, Allāh ﷻ says, **"The mountains will become like coloured cotton wool."** Even though they are symbols of stability, the mountains will fly about like wool on the Day of Qiyāmah. Allāh ﷻ says in Sūrah Wāqi'ah,

$$\text{وَبُسَّتِ الْجِبَالُ بَسًّا ○ فَكَانَتْ هَبَاءً مُّنْبَثًّا ○}$$

And the mountains will be scattered to pieces and become like scattered dust.(56:5-6)

In Sūrah Takwīr, it says,

$$\text{وَإِذَا الْجِبَالُ سُيِّرَتْ ○}$$

When the mountains are made to fly about (81:3)

If this is to be the state of the gigantic mountains the likes of Everest, Himalayas and K2, then one cannot imagine or comprehend the shock and disorientation that the rest of the creation will experience.

Allāh ﷻ says that the mountains are of different colours, as Allāh

🏵 says in Sūrah Fātir,

$$\text{وَمِنَ الْجِبَالِ جُدَدٌ بِيضٌ وَّحُمْرٌ مُّخْتَلِفٌ أَلْوَانُهَا وَغَرَابِيبُ سُوْدٌ ۟}$$

"From the mountains there are different ridges, varying from white to red of different shades and some which are extremely black. (35:27)

Weighing of Deeds

After describing the advent of the Day of Judgement, Allāh 🏵 describes the condition on the plain of resurrection. Allāh 🏵 says, **"As for him whose scales are weighty , he shall be enjoying a life of happiness."** The people of Jannah shall be completely satisfied with their lives. They will have absolutely no hardship or worries in Jannah.

Those people whose scales will be weighty are the ones who will receive their record of good deeds in their right hand. Allāh 🏵 proclaims,

$$\text{فَأَمَّا مَنْ أُوْتِيَ كِتَابَهُ بِيَمِيْنِهِ فَيَقُوْلُ هَاؤُمُ اقْرَءُوْا كِتَابِيَهْ ۟ إِنِّيْ ظَنَنْتُ أَنِّيْ مُلَاقٍ}$$
$$\text{حِسَابِيَهْ ۟ فَهُوَ فِيْ عِيْشَةٍ رَّاضِيَةٍ ۟ فِيْ جَنَّةٍ عَالِيَةٍ ۟ قُطُوْفُهَا دَانِيَةٌ ۟ كُلُوْا وَاشْرَبُوْا}$$
$$\text{هَنِيْئًا بِمَا أَسْلَفْتُمْ فِي الْأَيَّامِ الْخَالِيَةِ ۟}$$

"As for the one who receives his record (of actions) in his right hand (indicating that he is bound for Jannah), he will call out (to the others). "Come (everyone) and read my record!" I was always

convinced that I shall certainly meet my reckoning. "So he will enjoy a pleasing life in the lofty Jannah. It's fruits (the fruit of Jannah) are near at hand. At any time, a person will be able to have any one of the fruits that he desires for, without any effort. (The people will be told in Jannah). Eat and drink with all blessings as a reward for the (good) deeds that you sent during the days gone by (in the world)." (69:19-24)

On the other hand, "As for him whose scales are light, his abode shall be Hāwiya (pit). How will you know what this is. (It is) the blazing fire."

Those people whose scales will be light are the ones who will receive their record of bad deeds in their left hand.

Allāh ﷻ proclaims,

وَأَمَّا مَنْ أُوتِيَ كِتَابَهُ بِشِمَالِهِ فَيَقُولُ يَا لَيْتَنِي لَمْ أُوتَ كِتَابِيَهْ ۞ وَلَمْ أَدْرِ مَا حِسَابِيَهْ ۞ يَا لَيْتَهَا كَانَتِ الْقَاضِيَةَ ۞ مَا أَغْنَى عَنِّي مَالِيَهْ ۞ هَلَكَ عَنِّي سُلْطَانِيَهْ ۞ خُذُوهُ فَغُلُّوهُ ۞ ثُمَّ الْجَحِيمَ صَلُّوهُ ۞ ثُمَّ فِي سِلْسِلَةٍ ذَرْعُهَا سَبْعُونَ ذِرَاعًا فَاسْلُكُوهُ ۞ إِنَّهُ كَانَ لَا يُؤْمِنُ بِاللَّهِ الْعَظِيمِ ۞ وَلَا يَحُضُّ عَلَى طَعَامِ الْمِسْكِينِ ۞ فَلَيْسَ لَهُ الْيَوْمَ هَاهُنَا حَمِيمٌ ۞ وَلَا طَعَامٌ إِلَّا مِنْ غِسْلِينٍ ۞ لَّا يَأْكُلُهُ إِلَّا الْخَاطِئُونَ ۞

"As for the one who receives his record (of actions) in the left hand (indicating that he is bound for Jahannam, he will cry,

"Oh dear! If only I were not given my record... and I had not known my reckoning!" Alas! If only death had been my end (so that I would not have to witness this day!) My wealth (that I have greedily amassed) has not helped me (to attain salvation). "My kingship (The authority I had in this world for which I broke Allāh's command) has gone from me (and cannot help me here). (Addressing the angels of punishment, Allāh will say,) "Grab him (the one bound for Jahannam) and place a yoke around his neck! Then fasten him in a chain seventy cubit in length." Verily he did not believe in the Majestic Allāh and (let alone spending charity and feeding the poor) he did not even encourage (others towards) feeding the poor. There shall neither be any friend for him today (to assist him) nor any food except the filth (that) remains after washing (the puss and blood oozing from the wounds of the people of Jahannam). (It is a food that) only the sinners shall eat (in Jahannam)."(69:25-37)

Scholars have stated that the scales here in Sūrah Qāri'ah refer to the scales that measure Īmān and Kufr. Therefore, those who have Īmān shall be admitted into Jannah, while the disbelievers shall suffer eternally in Jahannam.

According to some commentators, the weighing of deeds here refers to the deeds of the believers. Therefore, those whose evil deeds are heavier will be admitted into Jahannam to be cleansed of their sins, while those whose good deeds are heavier will go straight to Jannah.

Sayyidunā Abdullāh Ibn Abbās ؓ has mentioned that those whose good deeds are heavier than their sins shall be admitted into Jannah, even if they are heavier by a single deed. On the other hand, those whose sins are heavier than their 'good' deeds, they will be doomed for Jahannam even if they are heavier by a single sin. He then recited the verses of Sūrah A'rāf where Allāh ﷻ says,

وَالْوَزْنُ يَوْمَئِذٍ الْحَقُّ فَمَنْ ثَقُلَتْ مَوَازِيْنُهُ فَأُولٰئِكَ هُمُ الْمُفْلِحُوْنَ وَمَنْ خَفَّتْ مَوَازِيْنُهُ فَأُولٰئِكَ الَّذِيْنَ خَسِرُوْا أَنْفُسَهُمْ بِمَا كَانُوْا بِآيَاتِنَا يَظْلِمُوْنَ

"The weighing on the day is the truth! As for him whose scale is light, these are the ones who have lost their souls because they were unjust towards Our verses." (7:8-9)

Sayidunā Abdullāh Ibn Abbās ؓ also mentioned that these scales will be sensitive to even an iotas weight of good or sin. Those whose good deeds are equal to their sins will be detained at 'Arāf' (the barrier between Jannah and Jahannam). They will be admitted in Jannah eventually. Those whose sins are heavier will also be eventually admitted into Jannah either by someone's intercession or after being cleansed of sins or purely by Allāh's ﷻ grace. A believer cannot remain eternally in Jahannam nor on A'rāf.

As for him whose scales are light, his abode shall be Hāwiya. How will you know what this is? (It is) the blazing fire.

37

Fire of Jahannam

The Arabic word "Umm" (translated above as "abode") literally refers to a mother. Jahannam will cling onto the people of Jahannam just as a mother clings onto her children. This is because these people clung to sins in this world in the same way. The Arabic word "Hāwiya" refers to something that falls. Jahannam is described as Hāwiya because of its extreme depth. Sayyidunā Utbah Ibn Ghazwān ﷺ narrates that a stone cast into Jahannam will continue falling for seventy years without reaching the bottom. (Muslim)

It is narrated from Sayyidunā Abū Hurairah ﷺ that the Holy Prophet ﷺ said,

نَارُ بَنِيْ آدَمَ الَّتِيْ يُوْقِدُوْنَ جُزْءٌ مِنْ سَبْعِيْنَ جُزْءًا مِّنْ نَارِ جَهَنَّمَ

The fire of the Children of Ādam that you all kindle is one part of the seventy parts of the fire of Hell.

In the narration of Imām Ahmad Ibn Hanbal ﷺ it says that Sayyidunā Abū Hurairah ﷺ relates from the Holy Prophet ﷺ who said,

إِنَّ أَهْوَنَ أَهْلِ النَّارِ عَذَابًا مَنْ لَهُ نَعْلَانِ يَغْلِيْ مِنْهُمَا دِمَاغُهُ

Verily, the person who will receive the lightest torment of the people of the Hellfire will be a man who will have two sandals that will cause his brain to boil. (Ahmad)

In the Hadīth of Bukhārī and Muslim, the Holy Prophet ﷺ said,

اِشْتَكَتِ النَّارُ إِلٰى رَبِّهَا فَقَالَتْ : رَبِّ أَكَلَ بَعْضِيْ بَعْضًا، فَأَذِنَ لَهَا بِنَفَسَيْنِ : نَفَسٍ فِي الشِّتَاءِ وَنَفَسٍ فِي الصَّيْفِ، فَأَشَدُّ مَا تَجِدُوْنَ مِنَ الحَرِّ، وَأَشَدُّ مَا تَجِدُوْنَ مِنَ الزَّمْهَرِيْرِ

The Hellfire complained to its Lord and said, "O Lord! Some parts of me devour other parts of me!" So He (Allāh ﷻ) permitted it to take two breaths: one breath in the summer and one breath in the winter. Thus, the most severe heat you experience in the summer is from its heat, and the most severe cold you experience in the winter is from its cold. (Bukhārī, Muslim).

In another Hadīth it is said,

إِذَا اشْتَدَّ الْحَرُّ فَأَبْرِدُوْا بِالصَّلَاةِ. فَإِنَّ شِدَّةَ الْحَرِّ مِنْ فَيْحِ جَهَنَّمَ

When the heat becomes intense, pray the prayer when it cools down, for indeed the intense heat is from the breath of Hell. (Bukhārī, Muslim)

39

Sūrah Takāthur (102)
In the name of Allāh, the Beneficent, the Merciful.

أَلْهَاكُمُ التَّكَاثُرُ ۝

(1) Rivalry in amassing wealth has destroyed you.

حَتّىٰ زُرْتُمُ الْمَقَابِرَ ۝

(2) Until you visit the graves.

كَلَّا سَوْفَ تَعْلَمُوْنَ ۝

(3) Never! You shall soon come to know.

ثُمَّ كَلَّا سَوْفَ تَعْلَمُوْنَ ۝

(4) Never! Soon you shall come to know.

كَلَّا لَوْ تَعْلَمُوْنَ عِلْمَ الْيَقِيْنِ ۝

(5) If you had certain knowledge (you would not have preoccupied yourself with rivalry).

لَتَرَوُنَّ الْجَحِيْمَ ۝

(6) (By Allāh) you will definitely see Jahannam.

ثُمَّ لَتَرَوُنَّهَا عَيْنَ الْيَقِيْنِ ۝

(7) (By Allāh) you will surely see it with the eye of certainty.

ثُمَّ لَتُسْأَلُنَّ يَوْمَئِذٍ عَنِ النَّعِيْمِ ۝

(8) Thereafter, on that day you will definitely be questioned about the bounties.

Connection between the Previous Sūrah and the Present one

In Sūrah Al-Qāri'ah, Allāh ﷻ mentions the catastrophes of the Day of Judgement and what mankind will encounter from the horrors and shock. In this Sūrah, Allāh ﷻ mentions those matters which people are pre-occupied with, in leading them to neglect the reality - the life after death.

Hence, a person should not engross himself in the worldly amusements that he forgets seeking the Hereafter.

Virtue of Sūrah Takāthur

Sayyidunā Abdullāh Ibn Umar ﷺ narrates that the Holy Prophet ﷺ once asked them, "Is there any of you who is able to recite a thousand verses of the Qur'ān daily?" The Sahābah ﷺ replied, "Who can have the strength to recite a thousand verses daily?" Thereupon the Holy Prophet ﷺ said, "Can you not recite أَلْهَاكُمُ التَّكَاثُرُ(Alhākumut-Takāthur (Sūrah Takāthur))?" This means that the reward for reciting Sūrah Takāthur equals the reward of reciting a thousand verses of the Qur'ān. (Baihaqī, Mishkāt)

Meaning of Takāthur

The Arabic word "Takāthur" refers to mutual rivalry between people in amassing wealth, a trait which is commonly witnessed in many people.

Sayyidunā Abdullāh Ibn Abbās ؓ and Hasan Basrī ؒ have assigned this interpretation to it. Qatādah ؒ says this word is also used in the sense of taking pride in the abundance of material goods. Sayyidunā Abdullāh Ibn Abbās ؓ relates that the Messenger of Allāh ﷺ recited this verse and explained its meaning, thus: "Acquiring wealth but not paying out of it the obligatory duties."

People vie with each other in amassing wealth and boast about their wealth to each other. Even though some people may not boast in front of others, this rivalry is ingrained in their mentality and they are always competing with others. Allāh ﷺ declares in Sūrah Hadīd,

$$ اِعْلَمُوْۤا اَنَّمَا الْحَيٰوةُ الدُّنْيَا لَعِبٌ وَّلَهْوٌ وَّزِيْنَةٌ وَّتَفَاخُرٌ بَيْنَكُمْ وَتَكَاثُرٌ فِي الْاَمْوَالِ وَالْاَوْلَادِ ۝ $$

"Know that the life of this world is merely play, futility, decoration, boasting among each other and rivalry in wealth and children." (57:20)

Being engrossed in competing with others in amassing wealth has caused man to neglect those actions that please Allāh ﷺ and had also caused him to forget that he is heading for the grave. In this manner, people pass through this world steeped in negligence and when they face the reality of the Ākhirah, they are bewildered and are lacking good deeds. Then the wealth they amassed will be useless to them. Allāh ﷺ refers to this when He says,

أَلْهَاكُمُ التَّكَاثُرُ ۞ حَتّٰى زُرْتُمُ الْمَقَابِرَ ۞

"Rivalry in amassing wealth has made you negligent until you reach your graves." (102:1-2)

Shān-e-Nuzūl: Cause of Revelation

Rivalry existed between the two tribes of Quraish, Banū Abd Manāf and Banū Sahm. On one occasion, both tribes boasted that they had a great number of noble and leaders. After counting, it was found that the number among the Banū Abd Manāf tribe was higher. Banū Sahm submitted that their deceased should also be included in the count because they had been part of their tribe. When the dead were counted, Banū Sahm emerged as victors by a few individuals. It was with reference to this that Allāh ﷻ revealed the verse, "Rivalry in amassing wealth has made you negligent until you reach your graves."

Warning Against Rivalry

Sayyidunā Abdullāh Ibn Zubair ﵁ whilst sitting on the pulpit at Makkah, delivering a Khutbah, he stated,

يَاۤ اَيُّهَا النَّاسُ اِنَّ النَّبِيَّ كَانَ يَقُوْلُ لَوْ اَنَّ ابْنَ اٰدَمَ اُعْطِيَ وَادِيًا مَلَأً مِنْ ذَهَبٍ اَحَبَّ اِلَيْهِ ثَانِيًا وَ لَوْ اُعْطِيَ ثَانِيًا اَحَبَّ اِلَيْهِ ثَالِثًا وَ لَا يَسُدُّ جَوْفَ ابْنِ اٰدَمَ اِلَّا التُّرَابُ (البخاري)

"O People! The Holy Prophet ﷺ used to say, "If the son of Ādam were given a valley of gold, he would love to have a second one; and if he were given the second one, he would love to have a third, for nothing fills the belly of Ādam's son except dust.

In the above Hadīth, the Holy Prophet ﷺ has warned us from mutual rivalry and amassing wealth which will be of no benefit to us in the Hereafter.

Sayyidunā Anas ﷺ relates from Sayyidunā Ubay Ibn Ka'b ﷺ who says,

كُنَّا نُرٰى هٰذَا فِي الْقُرْآنِ حَتّٰي نَزَلَتْ أَلْهَاكُمُ التَّكَاثُرُ

We considered this (the above Hadīth) as a saying from the Holy Qur'ān till Sūrah Takāthur was revealed.

It seems that the Holy Prophet ﷺ recited this verse and interpreted it in his own words. As a result, some of the Companions ﷺ were under the impression that the Prophetic words were part of the Holy Qur'ān. Later on, when the Sūrah was recited in it's entirety, it did not contain the Prophetic words. This made them realise that the Prophetic words were actually of an explanatory nature, and not part of the Holy Qur'ān.

Sayyidunā Abdullāh Ibn Shikhkhir ﷺ reports that one day he visited the Holy Prophet ﷺ whilst he was reciting Sūrah Takāthur and was saying,

يَقُوْلُ ابْنُ آدَمَ مَالِيْ مَالِيْ وَهَلْ لَكَ مِنْ مَالِكَ إِلَّا مَا أَكَلْتَ فَأَفْنَيْتَ أَوْ لَبِسْتَ فَأَبْلَيْتَ أَوْ
تَصَدَّقْتَ فَأَمْضَيْتَ وَفِيْ رِوَايَةٍ لِمُسْلِمٍ وَمَا سِوٰى ذٰلِكَ فَذَاهِبٌ وَتَارِكُهُ لِلنَّاس

The son of Ādam says, "My wealth, my wealth. But you do not reap any benefit from your wealth except for that which you ate and you finished it, or that which you clothed yourself with and you wore it out, or that which you gave as charity and you have spent it. In a narration of Muslim: Everything other than that will go away and he will leave it for other people (i.e. inheritors).

Imām Bukhāri 🕮 narrates from Sayyidunā Anas 🕮 that the Messenger of Allāh 🕮 said,

يَتْبَعُ الْمَيِّتَ ثَلَاثَةٌ فَيَرْجِعُ اثْنَانِ وَيَبْقَى مَعَهُ وَاحِدٌ يَتْبَعُهُ أَهْلُهُ وَمَالُهُ وَعَمَلُهُ فَيَرْجِعُ أَهْلُهُ وَ مَالُهُ وَيَبْقَى عَمَلُهُ (الْبُخَارِي)

"Three things follow the deceased person, and two of them return while one remain behind with him. The things which follow him are his family, his wealth and his deeds. His family and his wealth return while his deeds remain." (Bukhāri)

Imām Ahmad 🕮 recorded from Sayyidunā Anas 🕮 that the Holy Prophet 🕮 said,

يَهْرَمُ ابْنُ آدَمَ وَتَبْقَى مِنْهُ اثْنَتَانِ الْحِرْصُ وَالْأَمَلُ

"The son of Ādam becomes old, but two things remain with him; greed and hope. (Ahmad)

Types of Knowledge

Allāh ﷻ continues,

$$كَلَّا سَوْفَ تَعْلَمُونَ ۝$$

(3) "Never! (This rivalry will not benefit you)! Soon you will come to know the errors of your ways)!

Allāh ﷻ then reiterates,

$$ثُمَّ كَلَّا سَوْفَ تَعْلَمُونَ ۝$$

(4) "Again never! Soon you shall come to know!"

Allāh ﷻ says,

$$كَلَّا لَوْ تَعْلَمُونَ عِلْمَ الْيَقِينِ ۝$$

(5) "Never! If you had certain (definite) knowledge."

The word 'if' requires a principal clause that seems missing here; but the context suggests that the clause is the following, 'If you had certain knowledge of accountability on the Day of Judgement, you would not have engrossed yourselves in mutual competition in acquiring worldly goods and taking pride in their abundance.'
Thereafter Allāh ﷻ asserts,

$$لَتَرَوُنَّ الْجَحِيمَ ۞ ثُمَّ لَتَرَوُنَّهَا عَيْنَ الْيَقِينِ ۝$$

"(By Allāh) You will definitely see Jahannam. (By Allāh) You will surely see it with the eyes of certainty." (6-7)

When man sees the reality of the Hereafter for himself, he will truly be convinced by the truth of it.

The Three levels of Certainty

1. عِلْمُ الْيَقِيْن (Ilmul-Yaqīn): knowledge of certainty
2. عَيْنُ الْيَقِيْن (Aynul-Yaqīn): eye of certainty
3. حَقُّ الْيَقِيْن (Haqqul-Yaqīn): absolute truth

Describing the three levels of certainty, scholars mention that every living person has Ilmul-Yaqīn (absolute knowledge) about death. However, when man sees the angel of death approaching him he experiences Aynul Yaqīn (seeing death with the eye of certainty). Finally, Haqqul-Yaqīn (the irrefutable truth) is achieved once a person actually dies. (Rūhul-Ma'āni)

In terms of certainty, Haqqul-Yaqīn is the highest, then Aynul-Yaqīn and then Ilmul-Yaqīn. Sayyidunā Abdullah Ibn Abbās ؓ reports that when Prophet Mūsā علیہ السلام was on the Mount Tūr, his people started worshipping a calf. Allāh ﷻ informed him while he was still on the mountain. This piece of information did not affect Mūsā علیہ السلام so much. However, when he returned and saw the Banū Isrā'īl with his own eyes, worshipping the calf, he became so angered that the Tawrah involuntarily fell from his hands.

Several verses of the Holy Qur'ān warn people against preoccupying themselves with the commodities of this world in a manner that their lives revolve completely around these things and they live and die for them. Allāh ﷻ warns man that the consequence of such behaviour shall be that they see Jahannum and finally enter it. These verses remind man that this world is not everything and that death and the Hereafter are soon to follow.

Blessings of Allāh ﷻ

Allāh ﷻ concludes the Sūrah by stating,

$$ثُمَّ لَتُسْأَلُنَّ يَوْمَئِذٍ عَنِ النَّعِيمِ ۟$$

(8) Thereafter, on that day you will definitely be questioned about the bounties.

Everyone will be questioned whether they showed gratitude towards Allāh's ﷻ favours or did they misuse them and were ungrateful to Allāh ﷻ.

These favours are clearly and explicitly mentioned elsewhere in the Holy Qur'ān.

$$إِنَّ السَّمْعَ وَالْبَصَرَ وَالْفُؤَادَ كُلُّ أُولَٰئِكَ كَانَ عَنْهُ مَسْئُولًا ۟$$

"... Surely, questioning will take place with regard to the ears, the eyes and the heart.(17:36)

These organs and their faculties comprehend millions of blessings of Allāh ﷻ, and man will be questioned as to how he used them every moment of his life.

Sayyidunā Anas ؓ narrates that the Holy Prophet ﷺ said, "On the Day of Judgement, man will be brought forward like a lamb. He will then be presented before Allāh ﷻ, Who will ask, "Did I not grant you wealth and bounties? What did you do with these?" He will reply, "I accumulated it and multiplied it until it flourished. Then I left it all behind. Allow me to return and bring it all before you." The Holy Prophet ﷺ said, "Allāh ﷻ will say, 'Show me what you had sent ahead here to the Hereafter.' He will again reply, 'I accumulated it and multiplied it until it flourished. Allow me to return and bring it all before you.' It will then transpire that he was one who had not performed any good deeds on earth. He will then be flung into Jahannam." (Mishkāt)

Although it seems as if the concluding verse of Sūrah Takāthur addresses those who are destined for Jahannam, the general nature of the words make it impossible to rule out the possibility that every person will be questioned about the bounties that Allāh ﷻ blessed him with. Sayyidunā Abdullāh Ibn Mas'ūd ؓ narrates from the Holy Prophet ﷺ that a person will be unable to move from the place of reckoning until he answers five questions. These questions shall be:

1. In what way did he spend his life?
2. In what pursuits did he spend his youth?
3. How did he earn his wealth?
4. How did he spend his wealth?
5. Did he practise on the knowledge he had?   (Tirmizī)

Sayyidunā Abū Hurairah ؓ narrates that the first question that Allāh ﷻ will ask man concerning the bounties shall be: "Did I not give you good health?" and "Did I not quench your thirst with cold water?" (Tirmizī)

The Holy Prophet ﷺ always advised us to thank Allāh ﷻ for his bounties. Sayyidunā Abū Hurairah ؓ narrates, "Once, during a day or night, Allāh's Messenger ﷺ came out and found Sayyidunā Abū Bakr ؓ and Sayyidunā Umar ؓ. He said, 'What has brought you out of your homes at this hour?' They replied, 'Hunger, O Allāh's Messenger.' He said, ' By Him (Allāh) in Whose Hand my soul is, I too have come out for the same reason for which you have come out.' Then he said to them (both): 'Come along!' And he went along with them to a man from the Ansār, but they did not find him in his house. The wife of that man saw the Prophet ﷺ and said: 'You are welcome.' Allāh's Messenger ﷺ asked her (saying): 'Where is so-and-so?' She replied: 'He has gone to fetch some water for us.' In the meantime the Ansārī came, saw Allāh's Messenger ﷺ with his two Companions ؓ and said: 'All the praise and thanks be to Allāh ﷻ, today there is none superior to me as regards guests.'

Then he went and brought a part of a bunch of dates, some still green, some ripe, and some fully ripe and requested them to eat from it. He then took his knife (to slaughter a sheep for them), Allāh's Messenger ﷺ said to him, 'Beware! Do not slaughter a milk animal (an animal which gives milk).' So he slaughtered a sheep (prepared the meals from it's meat). They ate from that sheep and the bunch of dates and drank water. After they had finished eating and drinking to their fill, Allāh's Messenger ﷺ said to Sayyidunā Abu Bakr ﵁ and Sayyidunā Umar ﵁, 'By Him in Whose Hand my soul is, you will be asked about this treat on the Day of Judgement. He (Allāh ﷻ) brought you out of your homes with hunger and you are not returning to your homes till you have been blessed with this treat.

(Muslim)

Another narration reports that Rasūlullāh ﷺ, Sayyidunā Abu Bakr ﵁ and Sayyidunā Umar ﵁ once met an Ansāri Sahābi in his orchard. He served them a branch from a date palm from which they ate. When they asked for cold water, he served them some. Rasūlullāh ﷺ then told them that they will be questioned about this bounty on the Day of Judgement. Hearing this, Sayyidunā Umar ﵁ dropped the branch from his hand, causing all the dates to be scattered around. He then asked, "O Rasūlullāh, will we be questioned about this?" Rasūlullāh ﷺ confirmed that people will be questioned about every bounty except three. These are:

1.   A small piece of cloth used to cover the private parts.
2.   A piece of bread that appeases the hunger.

3.   A home to protect one from the heat and cold, which is so small that one has difficulty entering it.   (Mishkāt)

Sayyidunā Uthmān ؓ narrates from the Holy Prophet ﷺ that man has a right only to three things and to nothing else. These are:

1.   A house to live in.
2.   Sufficient clothing to conceal his private parts.
3.   Plain bread (without gravy) and water.   (Tirmizī)

Allāh ﷻ says in Sūrah Ibrāhīm,

وَإِنْ تَعُدُّوْا نِعْمَتَ اللّٰهِ لَا تُحْصُوْهَا ۗ إِنَّ الْإِنْسَانَ لَظَلُوْمٌ كَفَّارٌ

"If you try to count Allāh's bounties, you will never be able to do so. Indeed man is extremely unjust and very ungrateful." (14:34)

Man is extremely foolish. He humbles himself before people who give him things even though they may expect him to return the favour at some time. On the other hand, he refuses to humble himself before Allāh ﷻ, Who grants him countless favours without asking anything in return. Man refuses to prostrate to Allāh ﷻ and to fulfil His commands.

In a Hadīth of Bukhārī ﷺ, Sayyidunā Abdullāh Ibn Abbās ؓ narrates from the Holy Prophet ﷺ who said,

نِعْمَتَانِ مَغْبُوْنٌ فِيْهِمَا كَثِيْرٌ مِّنَ النَّاسِ اَلصِّحَّةُ وَالْفَرَاغُ

Two blessings concerning which many people are careless and oblivious; health and free time. (Bukhāri)

Sayyidunā Abū Hurairah ؓ narrates from the Holy Prophet ﷺ who stated,

يَقُوْلُ اللهُ عَزَّ وَ جَلَّ يَوْمَ الْقِيَامَةِ يَا ابْنَ آدَمَ حَمَلْتُكَ عَلَى الْخَيْلِ وَ الْإِبِلِ وَ زَوَّجْتُكَ النِّسَاءَ وَ جَعَلْتُكَ تَرْبَعُ وَ تَرْأَسُ فَأَيْنَ شُكْرُ ذٰلِكَ

"Allāh ﷻ will say on the Day of Judgement, 'O son of Ādam! I made you ride upon the horses and camels. I gave you women to marry and I made you reside and rule (on the earth). So where is the thanks for that?'" (Ahmad)

May Allāh ﷻ give us the Tawfīq (strength) to appreciate the blessings that Allāh ﷻ bestowed upon us. He proclaims, "If you show gratitude (for the favours I grant you), then I will definitely grant you (many) more (physical, spiritual and worldly favours).

May Allāh ﷻ increase His favours upon us in this world and the Hereafter. Āmīn!

Sūrah Asr
(The Time)

In the name of Allāh , the Most Compassionate, the Most Merciful.

وَالْعَصْرِ

(1)   By the oath of time.

إِنَّ الْإِنْسَانَ لَفِي خُسْرٍ

(2)   Verily man is at loss.

إِلَّا الَّذِيْنَ آمَنُوْا وَعَمِلُوا الصَّالِحَاتِ وَتَوَاصَوْا بِالْحَقِّ وَتَوَاصَوْا بِالصَّبْرِ

(3)   Except those who have Īmān, who do good deeds, who encourage each other towards the truth and who encourage each other to exercise patience.

Connection Between the Previous Sūrah and the Current Sūrah

In Sūrah Takāthur, it was mentioned that mankind destroys his invaluable life in greed and desires, in accumulating wealth and assets. In Sūrah Asr, Allāh ﷻ goes one step further and states that mankind even destroys his actual invaluable capital of life– which is time. Allāh ﷻ has granted man the invaluable capital of life, so that he may invest it in profitable business venture. If he invests his capital of life sensibly in good work there will be no limit to the profitable returns, but if he invests it unwisely in evil work, then let alone attracting profitable returns, he will even lose his capital.

In a Hadīth the Messenger of Allāh ﷺ says,

كُلُّ النَّاسِ يَغْدُو، فَبَائِعٌ نَفْسَهُ فَمُعْتِقُهَا، أَوْ مُوْبِقُهَا

When a person wakes up in the morning, he invests his soul or life in a business enterprise: some of the investors free or save the capital from loss and others destroy it.

The Holy Qur'ān itself has used the word Tijārah (business) to faith and righteous deeds, thus Allāh ﷺ says,

يَاأَيُّهَا الَّذِيْنَ آمَنُوْا هَلْ أَدُلُّكُمْ عَلَى تِجَارَةٍ تُنْجِيْكُمْ مِنْ عَذَابٍ أَلِيْمٍ

O you who believe! Shall I tell you about a trade that saves you from the painful punishment? (61:10)

Allāh ﷺ in the following verse answers,

تُؤْمِنُوْنَ بِاللهِ وَرَسُوْلِه وَتُجَاهِدُوْنَ فِيْ سَبِيْلِ اللهِ بِأَمْوَالِكُمْ وَأَنْفُسِكُمْ ذَلِكُمْ خَيْرٌ
لَكُمْ إِنْ كُنْتُمْ تَعْلَمُوْنَ

"(The trade is that you) Believe in Allāh and the Messenger and strive in Allāh's path with wealth and lives. This is best for you if you but knew. (61:11)

Virtues of Studying Sūrah Asr

Sayyidunā Ubaidullāh Ibn Hisn ؓ relates that whenever two Companions ؓ of the Holy Prophet ﷺ met, they would not part company until one of them has recited Sūrah Asr to the other. (Tabarāni)

The great Imām Shāfi'ī ﷺ says, "If the people were to ponder on this Sūrah, it would be sufficient for them."

Miracle of the Holy Qur'an

Sayyidunā Amr Ibnul-Ās ﷺ went to visit Musailamah Kazzāb after the prophethood of the Holy Prophet ﷺ and before Amr had accepted Islām. Upon his arrival, Musailamah said to him, "What has been revealed to your friend (Muhammad) during this time?"

Sayyidunā Amr ﷺ said, "A short and concise Sūrah has been revealed to him." Musailamah then said, "What is it?" Sayyidunā Amr ﷺ replied,

وَالْعَصْرِ . إِنَّ الْإِنْسَانَ لَفِي خُسْرٍ . إِلَّا الَّذِيْنَ آمَنُوْا وَعَمِلُوا الصَّالِحَاتِ وَتَوَاصَوْا بِالْحَقِّ وَتَوَاصَوْا بِالصَّبْرِ .

"By the oath of time, verily man is at loss. Except those who have Īmān, who do good deeds, who encourage each other towards the truth and who encourage each other to exercise patience."

So, Musailamah thought for a while, then he said, "Indeed something similar has been revealed to me." Sayyidunā Amr ﷺ asked him, "What is it?" He replied, O Wabr (a small, furry mammal). O Wabr! You are only two ears and a chest and the rest of you is digging and burrowing." Then he said, "What do you think O

Amr?" So Sayyidunā Amr ﷺ said to him, By Allāh ﷻ! Verily, you know that I know you are lying."

Wabr is a small animal that resembles a cat, and the largest thing on it is its ears and its torso, while the rest of it is ugly. Musailamah intended by the composition of these nonsensical verses to produce something that would oppose the Qur'ān, yet it was not even convincing to the idol worshipper of that time.

Relationship Between Time and Human Loss

The first point we need to analyse here is the relationship between the oath of time and its subject, because there needs to be a relationship between an oath and its subject.

The commentators generally state that all conditions of man, his growth and development , his movements, his actions and morality all take place within the space of 'Time'. Man will lose the capital of his existence. Seconds, minutes, hours, days, month and years of life pass quickly, spiritual and material potentialities decline and abilities fade. Man is like a person who possesses great capital and, without his permission everyday, a portion of that capital is taken away. This is the nature of life in this world, the nature of continual loss.

How well this has been put poetically,

$$حَيَاتُكَ اَنْفَاسٌ تُعَدُّ فَكُلَّمَا مَضَى نَفَسٌ مِنْهَا اِنْتَقَصَتْ بِهِ جُزْءًا$$

"Your life comprises a few breaths that can be counted, when one of them is sent out, a part of your life has diminished.

The Urdu poet says,

ہو رہی ہے عمر مثل برف کم

چپکے چپکے رفتہ رفتہ دم بدم

"Life is passing by, like the melting of ice very quietly, slowly slowly, breath by breath.

The great Sahābi, Sayyidunā Abū Dardā ؓ and the great Tābi'ī, Hasan Al-Basri ؒ said,

يَا ابْنَ اٰدَمَ اِنَّمَا اَنْتَ اَيَّامٌ فَاِذَا ذَهَبَ يَوْمٌ ذَهَبَ بَعْضُكَ

O Son of Ādam! You are but (a collection of) days: when a day goes, a part of you goes.

Imām Shāfi'ī ؒ says,

اَلْوَقْتُ سَيْفٌ فَاِنْ لَمْ تَقْطَعْهُ قَطَعَكَ

"Time is a sword. If you do not cut it (by utilising it in good deeds), it will definitely cut you.

When someone asked to speak to one of our pious predecessors, he said, "Stop the sun in its orbit for a while, only then (will I have free time) in which to converse."

A day that has passed will never return. Every morning at sunrise, the day says,

$$\text{مَنِ اسْتَطَاعَ أَنْ يَّعْمَلَ فِيْ خَيْرٍ فَلْيَعْمَلْهُ فَإِنِّيْ غَيْرُ مُكَرَّرٍ عَلَيْكُمْ أَبَدًا}$$

Whoever is able to do some good should do it, for I will never return to you. (Baihaqi)

A poet says,

عمر دراز مانگ کر لائے تھے چار دن

دو آرزو میں کٹ گئے دو انتظار میں

"After asking for a long life, you come with a short life. Half was spent in aspirations, and the other half in waiting."

How aptly Khawāja Azīzul Hasan Majzūb ☙, the senior disciple of Hakīmul-Ummah Shaykh Ashraf Alī Thānwi ☙ has drawn the complete picture of mans life in his spiritual poetry,

تجھے پہلے بچپن نے برسوں کھلایا, جوانی نے پھر تجھ کو مجنون بنایا

بڑھاپے نے پھر آ کے کیا کیا ستایا, اجل تیرا کردے گی بلکل صفایا

جگہ جی لگانے کی دنیا نہیں ہے, یہ عبرت کی جا ہے تماشا نہیں ہے

Initially, childhood delighted you with play for several years. Thereafter, youth made you insane. Then, old age, how it harassed you! Finally, death will completely annihilate you. This world is not a place of attachment. It is a place to take lesson, and is not a place of entertainment.

The Only Regret

Even after entering Jannah and being granted all the blessings of Jannah, the residents of Jannah will feel remorse upon the time they wasted in negligence whilst in this world.
The Noble Prophet ﷺ said,

لَيْسَ يَتَحَسَّرُ أَهْلُ الْجَنَّةِ إِلَّا عَلَى سَاعَةٍ مَرَّتْ بِهِمْ لَمْ يَذْكُرُوا اللَّهَ فِيْهَا

"The people of Jannah (after entering Jannah) will have no remorse over anything other than the time spent without remembering Allāh ﷻ. (Baihaqi, Tabarāni)

Before death strikes, we need to value our life. How, aptly it was inscribed on a gravestone.

يَا وَاقِفُ عِنْدَ قَبْرِيْ لَا تَتَعَجَّبُ مِنْ اَمْرِيْ
بِالْاَمْسِ كُنْتُ مِثْلَكَ وَغَدًا تَكُوْنُ مِثْلِيْ

"O the one standing in front of my grave, don't be astonished at my condition, yesterday I was like you, tomorrow you will become like me."

We need to resolve from today, that Inshā Allāh, we will no longer waste our time, not even a second in futile acts, and that we will invest every second in doing beneficial actions.

Beneficial Advice

Here are some beneficial points of guidance that are tried and tested and derived from the teaching of our pious predecessors. We should try to implement them in our lives in order to gain maximum benefit from our time.

1. Organise our time

Our elders were very particular about scheduling their time effectively, for it prevents time from being wasted. Therefore, we should make a programme for the whole day and night in the form of a timetable and adhere to it strictly. At any particular time, do only what you have assigned for that time and do not delay anything from its appointed time.

Do not put anything off until tomorrow, for tomorrow is simply a deception and a diversion. So make a habit of completing every task at its appointed time. In fact, strive for the enthusiasm to do tomorrow's task today and today's now.

2. Abstain from futile activities

Before doing anything, we should ask ourselves if it will be beneficial for our worldly life and our life in the Hereafter. If the answer is no, then we should stay away from it, though the action itself might not be harmful, but to spend a portion of life in an activity that is of no use in this world or the Hereafter is in fact a loss. No one would spend money on something that brings no benefit.

The famous Hadīth says,

مِنْ حُسْنِ إِسْلَامِ الْمَرْءِ تَرْكُهُ مَا لَا يَعْنِيهِ

"It is from the excellence of an individual's Islām that he leaves Lā Ya'nī (those things which do not benefit him)."

If that should be the situation regarding those things which do not benefit us, how can there be any justification for spending time on things that are harmful in this world or the Hereafter? Sins and disobedience to Allāh ﷻ brings harm in both worlds, so we need to save ourselves from them.

3. Unnecessary Gatherings

We should save ourselves from spending time in unnecessary gatherings. Nowadays, we not only engage in useless, futile talk in our gatherings, we also indulge in major sins such as backbiting and slander during weddings, or while visiting friends and colleagues. Brothers and sisters assemble for hours on end and waste time in useless talk.

4. Safeguarding the tongue

The poet says,

مَا نَدِمْتُ عَلَى السُّكُوْتِ أَبَدًا وَلَكِنْ نَدِمْتُ عَلَى الْكَلَامِ مِرَارًا

"I never regretted upon observing silence. But I have repeatedly regretted on speaking carelessly."

We need to learn to observe silence and not to speak without necessity. We need to control our tongue and think before we speak. Be brief in our speech and weigh our words before speaking.

5. Muhāsabah (Self-Reckoning)

We need to fix a time daily, preferably before retiring to bed and do Muhāsabah of the past 24 hours, so we know how our time is being spent. Through this, we will realise how much is being lost, and how much is being gained. If it has been spent in wrong avenues, then repent and make a firm resolution to keep away from such things in the future.

Verily Man is at Loss

Coming back to the verse of the Holy Qur'ān, **"Verily man is at loss."**

If man looks back in time and studies the history of past nations, it will become clear to him that most people have destroyed their lives by wasting their time in this world.

Since "Time" is a man's capital of life, the man himself is the trader. Under normal circumstances, his capital is not a frozen thing that may be kept for a while and used up later when the need arises. The capital is actually fluid or flowing all the time, every minute and every second. Man needs to be very wise, intelligent and cautious so that he is able to swiftly and readily reap the profit from a flowing capital. One of our pious predecessors said, I understood and learnt the meaning of this verse from an ice-seller whose trade required utmost diligence, and if he were neglectful for a moment, his entire capital will melt away.

This is why the verse has sworn an oath by time to indicate that it is a melting capital, and the only way to escape loss is to make every moment of one's life valuable and use it for the four actions mentioned in Sūrah Asr.

Four Actions

1.   Belief
2.   Good deeds
3.   Encourage others towards the truth
4.   Encourage others to exercise patience

People with these four attributes do not have to fear suffering any loss in the hereafter.

Belief and good deeds are related to each individual, but the latter two relates to the wider society. Hence, this Sūrah makes it clear that it is not sufficient for a person to be concerned about his spiritual condition only. He has to ensure that others also practice Dīn, especially his family and sub-ordinates. If he does not see to this, his wife, children and family will become a source of grief for him in the hereafter. The Noble Prophet ﷺ said,

اَلَا كُلُّكُمْ رَاعٍ وَكُلُّكُمْ مَسْؤُوْلٌ عَنْ رَعِيَّتِه

"Listen! Everyone is a shepherd and everyone of you will be questioned about his flock. (Bukhāri)

Sūrah Humazah
Those Who Search for Faults

In the name of Allāh, the Most Compassionate, the Most Merciful.

وَيْلٌ لِّكُلِّ هُمَزَةٍ لُّمَزَةٍ ۞

(1)   Destruction be for every person who searches for faults and mocks.

اَلَّذِيْ جَمَعَ مَالًا وَّعَدَّدَهُ ۞

(2)   Who amasses wealth and keeps meticulous count of it.

يَحْسَبُ أَنَّ مَالَهُ أَخْلَدَهُ ۞

(3)   He thinks that his wealth will keep him alive forever.

كَلَّا لَيُنْبَذَنَّ فِي الْحُطَمَةِ ۞

(4)   Never! He will certainly be thrown into the Crusher

وَمَا أَدْرَاكَ مَا الْحُطَمَةُ ۞

(5)   How will he know what the Crusher is?

$$نَارُ اللّٰهِ الْمُوۡقَدَةُ ۟ ۝$$

(6)   (It is) Allāh's kindled fire.

$$اَلَّتِىۡ تَطَّلِعُ عَلَى الۡاَفۡئِدَةِ ۝$$

(7)   Which penetrates the hearts.

$$اِنَّهَا عَلَيۡهِمۡ مُّؤۡصَدَةٌ ۝$$

(8)   It will certainly be locked over them.

$$فِىۡ عَمَدٍ مُّمَدَّدَةٍ ۝$$

(9)   In extended pillars.

Connection Between the Previous Sūrah and the Present Sūrah

In Sūrah Asr, Allāh ﷻ warns mankind from wasting his life and explains to him to safeguard and preserve it with four actions. In Sūrah Humazah, Allāh ﷻ mentions some evil traits which destroys human's humanity and his actual existence in the category of noble men. By perpetrating these evils sins, he destroys the true human nature with which Allāh ﷻ has sent him.

In Sūrah Asr, Allāh ﷻ mentions that man is at total loss and in this Sūrah, Allāh ﷻ mentions the ultimate result and abode of those people who will endure that loss.

Shān-e-Nuzūl—Cause of Revelation

Sūrah Humazah is a Makki Sūrah comprising of nine verses. This Sūrah was revealed regarding three staunch disbelievers and enemies of the Holy Prophet 🕌, Ās Ibn Wā'il, Walīd Ibn Mughīrah and Akhnas Ibn Sharīk. These three individuals were on the forefront in backbiting, slandering, taunting and mocking the Holy Prophet 🕌 and the believers. Allāh ﷻ informs them exclusively and the entire mankind generally regarding the ultimate consequences of these evil sins.

Humazah and Lumazah

The two words Humazah and Lumazah have been interpreted in different ways.

1.   Both words have one meaning and the repetition is for emphasis i.e. a person who constantly perpetrates this evil act. Hence words are from the chapter of فُعَلَة which comes for exaggeration.

2.   Humazah is used for a person who taunts and ridicules someone in his presence and Lumazah is used for an individual who does it in the absence of that person.

3.   Humazah is a person who belittles and taunts people with his hands, eyes and brows and Lumazah is a person who belittles and mocks a person verbally.

In brief, both of these words refer to people who search for faults in other people, who backbite, who ridicule, who speak evil of others, who condemn others, who laugh at others and who poke fun at the others physically, verbally or by indication (such as winking).

Allāh emphatically states in Sūrah Hujurāt, **"O you who have Īmān; men should not mock other men for perchance they may be better than them. Neither should any woman mock other women, perchance they may be better than them. Never find fault nor defame each other and do not call each other names. Of sin after Īmān is indeed evil. Those who do not repent are indeed oppressors."**

"O you who have Īmān! Refrain from excessive assumption. Verily, some assumptions are a sin. Never spy and never backbite each other. Does any of you like to eat the flesh of his dead brother, which you detest. Fear Allāh, Allāh is Most Pardoning, Most Merciful." (49:11-12)

In Sūrah Qalam, Allāh says, **"So do not obey every person who excessively swears an oath, who is disgraced, who searches for the faults of others, who excels in carrying tales." (68:10-11)**

In Sūrah Tawbah, Allāh condemns such actions, **"Of them are those who ridicule you concerning charity. (9:58)**

Punishment of Slandering and Backbiting

Sayyidunā Abdullāh Ibn Abbās ؓ says,

مَرَّ رَسُولُ اللهِ صَلَّى اللهُ عَلَيْهِ وَسَلَّمَ بِحَائِطٍ مِّنْ حِيْطَانِ مَكَّةَ أَوِ الْمَدِيْنَةِ، فَسَمِعَ صَوْتَ
إِنْسَانَيْنِ يُعَذَّبَانِ فِيْ قُبُوْرِهِمَا، فَقَالَ رَسُولُ اللهِ صَلَّى اللهُ عَلَيْهِ وَسَلَّمَ : "يُعَذَّبَانِ، وَمَا
يُعَذَّبَانِ فِيْ كَبِيْرٍ". ثُمَّ قَالَ: "بَلَى، كَانَ أَحَدُهُمَا لَا يَسْتَتِرُ مِنْ بَوْلِهِ، وَكَانَ الْآخَرُ يَمْشِيْ
بِالنَّمِيْمَةِ". ثُمَّ دَعَا بِجَرِيْدَةٍ فَكَسَرَهَا كِسْرَتَيْنِ فَوَضَعَ، فَقِيْلَ لَهُ: لِمَ فَعَلْتَ هٰذَا؟
قَالَ: "لَعَلَّهُ يُخَفَّفُ عَنْهُمَا مَالَمْ يَيْبَسَا

Once the Holy Prophet ﷺ, while passing through one of the gardens of Madīnah or Makkah heard the voices of two individuals who were being tortured in their graves. The Holy Prophet ﷺ said, "These two people are being tortured not for a major sin (to avoid). The Holy Prophet ﷺ then added, "yes, yes! (they are being tortured for a major sin). Indeed, one of them never saved himself from being soiled with his urine while the other used to go about tale bearing. The Holy Prophet ﷺ then asked for a green branch (of a date palm tree), broke it into two pieces and put one on each grave. On being asked why he had done so, he replied, "I hope that their torture might be lessened, till these get dried.

Sayyidunā Hudhaifah ؓ narrates that the Holy Prophet ﷺ said,

لَا يَدْخُلُ الْجَنَّةَ قَتَّاتٌ

One who tells tales shall not enter Jannah. (Bukhāri)

Sayyidunā Abū Hurairah 🙵 narrates that the Holy Prophet 🙵 said,

إِيَّاكُمْ وَالظَّنَّ. فَإِنَّ الظَّنَّ أَكْذَبُ الحَدِيْثِ، وَلَا تَحَسَّسُوْا، وَلَا تَجَسَّسُوْا، وَلَا تَنَاجَشُوْا، وَلَا تَحَاسَدُوْا، وَلَا تَبَاغَضُوْا، وَلَا تَدَابَرُوْا، وَكُوْنُوْا عِبَادَاللهِ إِخْوَانًا

"Beware of suspicion, for suspicion is the worst of false tales; do not search for faults, do not compete and do not practise Najsh (to offer a high price for something in order to allure another customer who is interested in the thing) and don't be jealous of another and don't hate one another, and do not desert one another, and be servants of Allāh 🙵 as brothers. (Bukhāri)

Sayyidunā Abdur-Rahmān Ibn Ghanam 🙵 and Sayyidah Asmā Bint Yazīd 🙵 narrates that the Holy Prophet 🙵 said, "The best servant of Allāh 🙵 are those who remind you of Allāh 🙵 when you see them. The worst servants of Allāh 🙵 are those who carry tales, who cast enmity between friends and who desire that harm should come to those who stay away from evil. (Mishkāt)

Sayyidunā Abdullāh Ibn Umar 🙵 narrates that the Holy Prophet 🙵 said, "That person cannot be a Mu'min who mocks, who curses, who is vulgar and who carries out indecent acts. (Mishkāt)

Amassing Wealth

Recounting another evil practice of the person who searches for the faults of others, Allāh 🙵 says that he also amasses wealth and keeps meticulous count of it. This trait betrays the person's extreme love for material wealth. When a person is engrossed with material wealth, he has no regard for Halāl and Harām when earning. He will leave no stone unturned to make money even though he has to usurp the wealth of another person or forsake his Farāidh and Wājibāt in the process. In addition to this, such a person regards material wealth as everything. Although he knows that he will have to die, he behaves as if his wealth will be of use to him forever. Referring to this behaviour, Allāh ﷻ says, he thinks that his wealth will keep him alive forever.

In a Hadīth, the Holy Prophet ﷺ says,

$$ لُعِنَ عَبْدُ الدِّيْنَارِ وَلُعِنَ عَبْدُ الدِّرْهَمِ $$

"Curse upon the servant of Dīnār and curse upon the servant of Dirham (i.e. he is always preoccupied with the amassing of money that he is as though he worships the money instead of Allāh ﷻ who is his real Creator)

Sayyidah Asmā ﷢ says that the Holy Prophet ﷺ said to her,

$$ لَا تُوْكِيْ فَيُوْكَى عَلَيْكِ $$

"Do not withhold your money, (for if you do so) Allāh ﷻ would withhold His blessings from you." (Bukhāri)

Those who accumulate wealth and do not spend in the path of Allāh ﷻ whether it is Zakāt, Sadaqah or helping the needy then there is severe warning and punishment awaiting for those people.

Sayyidunā Abū Hurairah ﷺ narrates that the Holy Prophet ﷺ said,

مَنْ آتَاهُ اللّٰهُ مَالًا فَلَمْ يُؤَدِّ زَكَاتَهُ, مُثِّلَ لَهُ يَوْمَ الْقِيَامَةِ شُجَاعًا أَقْرَعَ لَهُ زَبِيْبَتَانِ يُطَوَّقُهُ يَوْمَ الْقِيَامَةِ, ثُمَّ يَأْخُذُ بِلَهْزَمَتَيْهِ يَعْنِيْ شِدْقَيْهِ ثُمَّ يَقُوْلُ: أَنَا مَالُكَ أَنَا كَنْزُكَ

"Whoever is made wealthy by Allāh ﷺ and does not pay the Zakāt of his wealth, then on the Day of Resurrection his wealth will be made like a bald-headed poisonous male snake with two black spots over the eyes (or two poisonous glands in its mouth). The snake will encircle his neck and bite his cheeks and say, "I am your wealth, I am your treasure."

Mentioning the plight of the people of Hell, Allāh ﷺ says, "**As for the one who receives his record (of actions) in the left hand (indicating that he is bound for Jahannam) he will cry, "Oh! Dear! If only I were not given my record and I had not known my reckoning. Alas! If only death had been my end (so that I would not have witnessed this day)!"**

"**My wealth (that I greedily amassed) has not helped me (to attain salvation). My kingship (the authority I had in this world for which I broke Allāh's commands) has been lost for me (and cannot help me here)."**

Allāh ﷺ emphatically negates the false notion when He says that the wealth will keep him alive forever. He states, "Never." Neither will the person live forever in this world nor will his wealth remain forever. Mentioning the plight of such a person, Allāh says, "he will certainly be thrown into the crusher. How will you know what the crusher is. (It is) Allāh's kindled fire which penetrates the hearts." The fire of Jahannam is so intense that it will not only burn the bodies of people but it will reach their hearts. Although this is sufficient to kill a person in this world, the people of Jahannam will not die.

Allāh says in Sūrah Nisā, **"Whenever their skins melt away, We shall exchange them for fresh skins so that they may taste the torment." (4:56)**

A verse of Sūrah A'lā states, **"He (the person in Jahannam) will then neither die there nor live. (87:13)**

Fire of Jahannam

Describing the Hellfire, the Holy Prophet said,

نَارُكُمْ جُزْءٌ مِّنْ سَبْعِيْنَ جُزْءًا مِّنْ نَارِ جَهَنَّمَ ، قِيْلَ: يَا رَسُوْلَ اللهِ، إِنْ كَانَتْ لَكَافِيَةً، قَالَ: فُضِّلَتْ عَلَيْهَا بِتِسْعَةٍ وَسِتِّيْنَ جُزْءًا كُلُّهُنَّ مِثْلُ حَرِّهَا

"Your (ordinary) fire is one of 70 parts of the Hellfire." Someone asked, "O Messenger of Allāh! This (ordinary) fire would have been sufficient (to torture the disbelievers)." Allāh's Messenger said, "The Hell fire has 69 parts more than the ordinary (worldly) fire, each part is as hot as this (worldly) fire. (Bukhāri)

Sayyidunā Nu'mān 🙵 narrates, I heard the Holy Prophet 🙵 saying,

اِنَّ أَهْوَنَ أَهْلِ النَّارِ عَذَابًا يَوْمَ الْقِيَامَةِ لَرَجُلٌ، تُوْضَعُ فِيْ أَخْمَصِ قَدَمَيْهِ جَمْرَةٌ، يَغْلِيْ مِنْهَا دِمَاغُهُ

The person who will have the least punishment from among the people of (Hell) fire on the Day of Judgement will be a man under whose arch of the feet a smouldering ember will be placed so that his brain will boil from it. (Bukhāri)

The phrase 'Allāh's kindled fire' makes it clear that the fire of Jahannam has already been kindled and will be ready before people are thrown into it. Sayyidunā Abū Hurairah 🙵 narrates from the Holy Prophet 🙵 that the fire of Jahannam was kindled for a thousand years until it became red. It was then kindled for another thousand years until it became white. It was then kindled for another thousand years until it became black. It is now black and dark. (Tirmizī)

Thābit Al-Bunāni 🙵 said, "It will burn them all the way to their hearts while they are still alive." Then he said, "Indeed the torment will reach them." Then he cried. Muhammad Ibn Ka'b 🙵 said, "It (the fire) will devour every part of his body until it reaches his heart and comes to the level of his throat, then it will return to his body.

Further describing the Fire of Jahannam, Allāh 🙵 says, **"It will cer-**

tainly be locked over them in extended pillars." The doors of Jahannam will be locked and there will be no escape.

Sayyidunā Abdullāh Ibn Abbās ﷺ has mentioned that the doors of Jahannam will be sealed with pillars. Allāmah Qurtubi ﷺ has reported that the pillars refer to the yokes that will be placed on their necks so that they cannot escape. Other commentators mention that the pillars refer to the large flames of Jahannam which will scorch the people there, making it impossible for them to escape.

In Tafsīr Azīzi, Shāh Abdul-Azīz ﷺ says, "The fire will be locked in their organs and limbs that it will not escape from them and neither would cold air be able to enter the limbs. Likewise, the body parts will be heavily shackled lest it makes movements which might ease the punishment for a short while.

May Allāh ﷺ save us from the punishment of Hell and save us from the wrath of Allāh ﷺ. Āmīn.

Kanzul Bāri

Kanzul Bāri provides a detailed commentary of the Ahādeeth contained in Saheeh al-Bukhāri. The commentary includes Imām Bukhāri's ﷺ biography, the status of his book, spiritual advice, inspirational accounts along with academic discussions related to Fiqh, its application and differences of opinion. Moreover, it answers objections arising in one's mind about certain Ahādeeth. Inquisitive students of Hadīth will find this commentary a very useful reference book in the final year of their Ālim course for gaining a deeper understanding of the science of Hadīth. **UK RRP: £15.00**

How to Become a Friend of Allāh ﷺ

The friends of Allāh ﷺ have been described in detail in the Holy Qur'ān and ĀHadīth. This book endeavours its readers to help create a bond with Allāh ﷺ in attaining His friendship as He is the sole Creator of all material and immaterial things. It is only through Allāh's ﷺ friendship, an individual will achieve happiness in this life and the Hereafter, hence eliminate worries, sadness, depression, anxiety and misery of this world. **UK RRP:**

Gems & Jewels

This book contains a selection of articles which have been gathered for the benefit of the readers covering a variety of topics on various aspects of daily life. It offers precious advice and anecdotes that contain moral lessons. The advice captivates its readers and will extend the narrowness of their thoughts to deep reflection, wisdom and appreciation of the purpose of our existence. **UK RRP: £4.00**

End of Time

This book is a comprehensive explanation of the three Sūrahs of Juzz Amma; Sūrah Takweer, Sūrah Infitār and Sūrah Mutaffifeen. This book is a continuation from the previous book of the same author, 'Horrors of Judgement Day'. The three Sūrahs vividly sketch out the scene of the Day of Judgement and describe the state of both the inmates of Jannah and Jahannam. Mufti Saiful Islām Sāhib provides an easy but comprehensive commentary of the three Sūrahs facilitating its understanding for the readers whilst capturing the horrific scene of the ending of the world and the conditions of mankind on that horrific Day. **UK RRP: £5.00**

Andalus (modern day Spain), the long lost history, was once a country that produced many great calibre of Muslim scholars comprising of Mufassirūn, Muhaddithūn, Fuqahā, judges, scientists, philosophers, surgeons, to name but a few. The Muslims conquered Andalus in 711 AD and ruled over it for eight-hundred years. This was known as the era of Muslim glory. Many non-Muslim Europeans during that time travelled to Spain to study under Muslim scholars. The remanences of the Muslim rule in Spain are manifested through their universities, magnificent palaces and Masājid carved with Arabic writings, standing even until today. In this book, Shaykh Mufti Saiful Islām shares some of his valuable experiences he witnessed during his journey to Spain. **UK RRP: £3.00**

Ideal Youth

This book contains articles gathered from various social media avenues; magazines, emails, WhatsApp and telegram messages that provide useful tips of advice for those who have the zeal to learn and consider changing their negative habits and behavior and become better Muslims to set a positive trend for the next generation. **UK RRP:£4:00**

Ideal Teacher

This book contains abundance of precious advices for the Ulamā who are in the teaching profession. It serves to present Islamic ethical principles of teaching and to remind every teacher of their moral duties towards their students. This book will Inshā-Allāh prove to be beneficial for newly graduates and scholars wanting to utilize their knowledge through teaching. **UK RRP:£4:00**

Ideal Student

This book is a guide for all students of knowledge in achieving the excellent qualities of becoming an ideal student. It contains precious advices, anecdotes of our pious predecessors and tips in developing good morals as a student. Good morals is vital for seeking knowledge. A must for all students if they want to develop their Islamic Knowledge. **UK RRP:£4:00**

Ideal Parents

This book contains a wealth of knowledge in achieving the qualities of becoming ideal parents. It contains precious advices, anecdotes of our pious predecessors and tips in developing good parenthood skills. Good morals is vital for seeking knowledge. A must for all parents . **UK RRP:£4:00**

Ideal Couple

This book is a compilation of inspiring stories and articles containing useful tips and life skills for every couple. Marriage life is a big responsibility and success in marriage is only possible if the couple know what it means to be an ideal couple. **UK RRP:£4:00**

Ideal Role Model

This book is a compilation of sayings and accounts of our pious predecessors. The purpose of this book is so we can learn from our pious predecessors the purpose of this life and how to attain closer to the Creator. Those people who inspires us attaining closeness to our Creator are our true role models. A must everyone to read. **UK RRP:£4:00**

Ideal Role Model

This book is a compilation of sayings and accounts of our pious predecessors. The purpose of this book is so we can learn from our pious predecessors the purpose of this life and how to attain closer to the Creator. Those people who inspires us attaining closeness to our Creator are our true role models. A must everyone to read. **UK RRP:£4:00**

Bangladesh– A Land of Natural Beauty

This book is a compilation of our respected Shaykh's journeys to Bangladesh including visits to famous Madāris and Masājid around the country. The Shaykh shares some of his thought provoking experiences and his personal visits with great scholars in Bangladesh. **UK RRP: £4.00**

Pearls from the Qur'an

This series begins with the small Sūrahs from 30th Juzz initially, unravelling its heavenly gems, precious advices and anecdotes worthy of personal reflection. It will most definitely benefit both those new to as well as advanced students of the science of Tafsīr. The purpose is to make it easily accessible for the general public in understanding the meaning of the Holy Qur'ān. **UK RRP: £10.00**

When the Heavens Split

This book contains the commentary of four Sūrahs from Juzz Amma namely; Sūrah Inshiqāq, Sūrah Burūj, Sūrah Tāriq and Sūrah A'lā. The first two Sūrahs contain a common theme of capturing the scenes and events of the Last Day and how this world will come to an end. However, all four Sūrahs mentioned, have a connection of the journey of humanity, reflection on nature, how nature changes and most importantly, giving severe warnings to mankind about the punishments and exhorting them to prepare for the Hereafter through good deeds and refraining from sins. **UK RRP: £4.00**

The Lady who Spoke the Qur'ān

The Holy Prophet ﷺ was sent as a role model who was the physical form of the Holy Qur'ān. Following the ways of the Holy Prophet ﷺ in every second of our lives is pivotal for success. This booklet tells us the way to gain this success. It also includes an inspirational incident of an amazing lady who only spoke from the Holy Qur'an throughout her life. We will leave it to our readers to marvel at her intelligence, knowledge and piety expressed in this breath-taking episode. **UK RRP:£3:00**

Dearest Act to Allāh

Today our Masājid have lofty structures, engraved brickworks, exquisite chandeliers and laid rugs, but they are spiritually deprived due to the reason that the Masājid are used for social purposes including backbiting and futile talk rather than the performance of Salāh, Qur'ān recitation and the spreading of true authentic Islamic knowledge. This book elaborates on the etiquettes of the Masjid and the importance of Salāh with Quranic and prophetic proofs along with some useful anecdotes to emphasize their importance. **UK RRP:£3:00**

on't Delay Your Nikāh

Iarriage plays an important role in our lives. It is a commemoration of the un-
•n of two strangers who will spend the rest of their remaining lives with one
nother. Marriage ought to transpire comfort and tranquillity whereby the cou-
le share one another's sorrow and happiness. It is strongly recommended that
ur brothers and sisters read and benefit from this book and try to implement it
•to our daily lives in order to once more revive the Sunnah of the Holy Prophet
• on such occasions and repel the prevalent sins and baseless customs.

UK RRP:£3:00

Miracle of the Holy Qur'ān

The scholars of Islām are trying to wake us all up, however, we are busy dreaming of the present world and have forgotten our real destination. Shaykh Mufti Saiful Islām Sāhib has been conducted Tafsīr of the Holy Qur'ān every week for almost two decades with the purpose of reviving its teachings and importance. This book is a transcription of two titles; Miracle of the Holy Qur'ān and The Revelation of the Holy Qur'ān, both delivered during the weekly Tafsīr sessions. **UK RRP:£3:00**

ou are what you Eat

ating Halāl and earning a lawful income plays a vital role in the acceptance of
ll our Ibādāt (worship) and good deeds. Mufti Saiful Islām Sāhib has presented
 discourse on this matter in one of his talks. I found the discourse to be very
eneficial, informative and enlightening on the subject of Halāl and Harām that
arifies its importance and status in Islām. I strongly recommend my Muslim
rothers and sisters to read this treatise and to study it thoroughly.

UK RRP:£3:00

Sleepers of the Cave

The Tafsīr of Sūrah Kahf is of crucial importance in this unique and challenging time we are currently living in. This book is evidently beneficial for all Muslims, more crucial for the general public. This is because Mufti Sāhib gives us extensive advice on how to act accordingly when treading the path of seeking knowledge. Readers will find amazing pieces of advice in terms of etiquettes regarding seeking knowledge and motivation, Inshā-Allāh. **UK RRP:£5:00**

Contentment of the Heart

The purification of the soul and its rectification are matters of vital importance which were brought by our Holy Prophet e to this Ummah. The literal meaning of Tazkiyah is 'to cleanse'. The genuine Sūfis assert that the foundation and core of all virtuous character is sincerity and the basis for all evil characteristics and traits is love for this world. This book endeavors to address certain spiritual maladies and how to overcome them using Islamic principles. **UK RRP:£5:00**

Contemporary Fiqh

This book is a selection of detailed *Fiqhi* (juridical) articles on contemporary legal issues. These detailed articles provide an in depth and elaborative response to some of the queries posted to us in our Fatawa department over the last decade. The topics discussed range between purity, domestic issues, Halāl and Harām, Islamic medical ethics, marital issues, rituals and so forth. Many of the juristic cases are unprecedented as a result of the ongoing societal changes and newly arising issues. **UK RRP:£6:00**

Ideal Society

In this book, 'Ideal Society' which is a commentary of Sūrah Hujurāt, Shaykh Mufti Saiful Islām Sāhib explains the lofty status of our beloved Prophet 🕌, the duties of the believers and general mankind and how to live a harmonious social life, which is free from evil, jealousy and vices. Inshā-Allāh, this book will enable and encourage the readers to adopt a social life which will ultimately bring happiness and joy to each and every individual.

UK RRP:£5:00

Quranic Wonders

The science of Tafsīr in itself is very vast, hence the compilation of these specific verses provides the reader with a simple and brief commentary. It is aimed to equip the reader with a small glimpse of the profound beauty of the Holy Qur'ān so that they can gain the passion to study further in depth. It is hoped that this will become a means of encouragement to increase the zeal and enthusiasm to recite and inculcate the teachings of the Holy Qur'ān into our daily lives. **UK RRP:£5:00**

Protection in the Grave

Sūrah Al-Mulk encapsulates the purpose of our creation - that we were created to live a life of obedience to our Lord and Creator. This can only be made to manifest through our good deeds which we perform solely for the sake of Allāh 🕮, in order to seek His pleasure. The Holy Prophet 🕮 told his Ummah to recite this Sūrah every night and learn this Sūrah by heart. The importance of this Sūrah is stressed due to the fact that the Holy Prophet 🕮 never slept until he had finished reciting this Sūrah. **UK RRP:£4:00**

Protection from Black Magic

These last ten Sūrahs are not only distinct in their meanings and message which will be discussed in this book, but also the fact that every Muslim should have these Sūrahs committed to memory as a minimum requirement in seeking refuge in Allāh 🕮 from all harm and evil, and every imperfection as well as seeking solace and peace in understanding His might and attributes. **UK RRP:£5:00**

urturing Children in Islam

ringing up children has never been an easy duty. The challenges do not t easier as they get older either. Our emotions and other priorities metimes hinder in nurturing our children, and as such, we fail to as st our children in reaching their potential by continually stumbling er our own perception of what we consider as ideal children. Our duty our children is not without accountability. Our neglect and lack of terest in our children will be held to task. **UK RRP:£5:00**

Best of Stories
Sūrah Yūsuf is more than just a story of one of our beloved Prophets ﷺ there is much wisdom and lessons to be learnt and understood. All the knowledge comes from our honourable Shaykh, inspiration and Ustādh Shaykh Mufti Saiful Islām Sāhib. May Allāh ﷻ shower Mufti Sāhib with mercy and accept the day in, day out effort he carries out in the work of Dīn. **UK RRP:£4:00**

Call of Nuh
For 950 years, Sayyidunā Nūh ﷺ persevered night and day in continuous succession in preaching the message; unwavering and relentless in his mission. Not once did he feel that his calling was in vain. He stood firm and resolute in continuing with the mission that he was sent with, in proclaiming the message of the oneness of Allāh ﷻ; year after year, decade upon decade, century after century, but this failed to convince the people of the truth. **UK RRP:£4:00**